BGE LEVEL 3 and 4

BUSINESS
COURSE BOOK

Reynolds, Morin and Wingate

First published in 2023 by:
Bright Red Publishing Ltd
Mitchelston Drive Business Centre
Kirkcaldy
KY1 3NB

A CIP record for this book is available from the British Library.

ISBN 9781906736934

With thanks to:
PDQ Digital Media Solutions Ltd, Bungay (layout).
Cover design and series book design by Caleb Rutherford – e i d e t i c.

Every effort has been made to seek all copyright-holders. If any have been overlooked, then Bright Red Publishing will be delighted to make the necessary arrangements.

Acknowledgements
Permission has been sought from all relevant copyright holders and Bright Red Publishing are grateful for the use of the following:

Microsoft, Word, Excel, Access and PowerPoint are trademarks of the Microsoft group of companies (pp 5, 100 & 101); Maxx-Studio/Shutterstock.com (pp 8–9); Ivelin Radkov/Shutterstock.com (pp 10, 24, 38, 52, 74, 90, 102, 114, 134, 147 top); jamesteohart/Shutterstock.com (pp 10, 24, 38, 52, 74, 90, 102, 114, 134, 147 middle); zirconicusso/Shutterstock.com (p 10); Virrage Images/Shutterstock.com (p 10); Irina Wilhauk/Shutterstock.com (p 12 top); Cronislaw/Shutterstock.com (p 12 bottom); docstockmedia/Shutterstock.com (p 13); Billion Photos/Shutterstock.com (p 15); Maxx-Studio/Shutterstock.com (p 16 top); ivan_kislitsin/Shutterstock.com (p 16 left); New Africa/Shutterstock.com (p 16 middle left); Virrage Images/Shutterstock.com (p 16 middle right); pilipphoto/Shutterstock.com (p 16 right); REDPIXEL.PL/Shutterstock.com (p 17 left); t.max/Shutterstock.com (p 17 middle left); Mr.Music/Shutterstock.com (p 17 middle right); Cast Of Thousands/Shutterstock.com (p 17 right); McLittle Stock/Shutterstock.com (pp 22–23); Rawpixel.com/Shutterstock.com (p 24); Tartila/Shutterstock.com (p 25 top); Jerome.Romme/Shutterstock.com (p 25 bottom); Advert reproduced by permission of KFC (p 26 left); Advert reproduced by permission of Nestlé S.A. Aero® is a registered trademark(s) of Société des ProduitsNestlé S.A. (p 26 middle); Advert reproduced by permission of Ben & Jerry's/Unilever (p 26 right); 13_Phunkod/Shutterstock.com (p 27 top); stoatphoto/Shutterstock.com (p 27 bottom); Logo reproduced by permission of Citroën UK/Stellantis N.V. (p 28); The NIKE ® swoosh logo © NIKE, Inc. (p 28); Logo reproduced by permission of Peugot UK/Stellantis N.V. (p 28); The adidas® logo © adidas AG (p 28); Logo reproduced by permission of Fred Perry Ltd. (p 28); Logo reproduced by permission of River Island Clothing Co. Limited (p 28); Logo reproduced by permission of Vauxhall UK/Stellantis N.V. (p 28); Logo and strapline i'm lovin it® reproduced by permission of McDonald's Restaurants Limited (p 28 bottom); Pringles packaging reproduced by permission of KELLOGG Company (p 29 left); Image reproduced by permission of Nestlé S.A. Smarties® is a registered trademark(s) of Société des ProduitsNestlé S.A. (p 29 right); Africa Studio/Shutterstock.com (p 30 & 34 bottom); Trueffelpix/Shutterstock.com (p 32); Sergey Nivens/Shutterstock.com (p 33 top); ML Robinson/Shutterstock.com (p 33 bottom); Parilov/Shutterstock.com (p 34 top); PX Media/Shutterstock.com (pp 36–37); miniwide/Shutterstock.com (p 38); two images fizkes/Shutterstock.com (p 39 top & middle); Sebastian Duda/Shutterstock.com (p 39 bottom); TheVisualsYouNeed/Shutterstock.com (p 41); tomertu/Shutterstock.com (p 42 top); northallertonman/Shutterstock.com (p 42 bottom); Prazis Images/Shutterstock.com (p 44); VGstockstudio/Shutterstock.com (p 45 top); wavebreakmedia/Shutterstock.com (p 45 bottom); Jason Winter/Shutterstock.com (p 46 top right); NAN728/Shutterstock.com (p 46 middle left); gabczi/Shutterstock.com (p 46 middle right); kpatyhka/Shutterstock.com (p 46 bottom left); 1000 Words/Shutterstock.com (p 46 bottom right); Nicola Forenza/Shutterstock.com (p 47 top); nimito/Shutterstock.com (p 47 bottom); Monster Ztudio/Shutterstock.com (pp 50–51); Kemal Taner/Shutterstock.com (p 52 middle right); stoatphoto/Shutterstock.com (p 52 bottom right); Nopparat Khokthong/Shutterstock.com (p 54 middle); Worranan Junhom/Shutterstock.com (p 54 bottom); Ground Picture/Shutterstock.com (p 56 top); Perfect Gui/Shutterstock.com (p 56 bottom); mavo/Shutterstock.com (p 57); stockfour/Shutterstock.com (p 58 top); Elena..D/Shutterstock.com (p 58 bottom); PopTika/Shutterstock.com (p 61); Teerasak Ladnongkhun/Shutterstock.com (p 62 top); Rawpixel.com/Shutterstock.com (p 62 middle); Doubletree Studio/Shutterstock.com (p 62 bottom); Maxx-Studio/Shutterstock.com (p 63); xavitgn/Shutterstock.com (p 65 top); viewimage/Shutterstock.com (p 65 middle); Logo reproduced by permission of Santander UK plc (p 65 bottom); Atstock Productions/Shutterstock.com (p 66); KUMOHD/Shutterstock.com (p 68 top); KUMOHD/Shutterstock.com (p 68 middle); Justin_Krug/Shutterstock.com (p 69 top); Kardasov Films/Shutterstock.com (p 69 middle); Avigator Fortuner/Shutterstock.com (pp 72–73); Image © Starbucks Corporation (p 74 middle left); P_WON/Shutterstock.com (p 74 bottom left); Image © Google. Google and the Google logo are trademarks of Google LLC (p 75); Travel mania/Shutterstock.com (p 76 top); p76 middle images clockwise: Lex0077/Shutterstock.com, Avigator Fortuner/Shutterstock.com, Fevziie/Shutterstock.com; p76 bottom images clockwise: Mr.PK/Shutterstock.com, barmalini/Shutterstock.com, PHOTOCREO Michal Bednarek/Shutterstock.com; Waldemarus/Shutterstock.com (p 77 top); picoStudio/Shutterstock.com (p 77 middle); The Fairtrade Mark is reproduced by permission of The Fairtrade Foundation (p 80 right); nullplus/Shutterstock.com (p 80 left); Victor Runov/Shutterstock.com (p 81); BUTENKOV ALEKSEI/Shutterstock.com (p 82); Bankoo/Shutterstock.com (p 83 right); STILLFX/Shutterstock.com (p 83 top); belekekin/Shutterstock.com (p 83 middle); RaffMaster/Shutterstock.com (p 83 bottom); Logo reproduced by permission of Oxfam International (p 86 top); Jevanto Productions/Shutterstock.com (p 86 middle); Jirapong Manustrong/Shutterstock.com (p 86 bottom); MNBB Studio/Shutterstock.com (p 87); 3rdtimeluckystudio/Shutterstock.com (pp 88–89); My Agency/Shutterstock.com (p 90 bottom); Everett Collection/Shutterstock.com (p 91 top); ian baigent-scales/Shutterstock.com (p 91 bottom); Ground Picture/Shutterstock.com (p 92 top); Lukas Bischoff Photograph/Shutterstock.com (p 92 middle); Daisy Daisy/Shutterstock.com (p 95); Antonio Guillem/Shutterstock.com (p 96); Wachiwit/Shutterstock.com (pp 98–99); Baker Jundip/Shutterstock.com (p 100 top); Top Popular Vector/Shutterstock.com (p 100 middle); BigTunaOnline/Shutterstock.com (p 101); Wachiwit/Shutterstock.com (p 114 bottom); PixieMe/Shutterstock.com (p 122); Dragon Images/Shutterstock.com (p 124); wavebreakmedia/Shutterstock.com (p 125); Niloo/Shutterstock.com (p 126); tartanparty/Shutterstock.com (p 127); Juice Flair/Shutterstock.com (p 128); BearFotos/Shutterstock.com (p 129); Pickadook/Shutterstock.com (p 130); HYS_NP/Shutterstock.com (p 131); Fusionstudio/Shutterstock.com (p 132 top); ShutterOK/Shutterstock.com (p 132 bottom); Karen Grigoryan/Shutterstock.com (p 133 top); TY Lim/Shutterstock.com (p 133 bottom); Stokkete/Shutterstock.com (p 134 bottom); Alhim/Shutterstock.com (p 135); Ground Picture/Shutterstock.com (p 136); Lukasz Libuszewski/Shutterstock.com (p 137); BearFotos/Shutterstock.com (p 138); maroke/Shutterstock.com (p 139); Pixel-Shot/Shutterstock.com (p 141); Stokkete/Shutterstock.com (p 142); Sergey Novikov/Shutterstock.com (p 143); Andrewshots/Shutterstock.com (p 144); INTREEGUE Photography/Shutterstock.com (p 145); Nach-Noth/Shutterstock.com (p 146); metamorworks/Shutterstock.com (p 147 bottom); JaySi/Shutterstock.com (p 148); Marcio Jose Bastos Silva/Shutterstock.com (p 149); Gilles Lougassi/Shutterstock.com (p 150).

Printed and bound in the UK.

CONTENTS

INTRODUCTION

INTRODUCING BRIGHT RED BGE BUSINESS

Welcome to the Bright Red Business Education textbook for the Broad General Education. This book should guide you through all the Outcomes and Benchmarks for Business Education for the Scottish Curriculum using active learning strategies. The book will also enable learners to develop literacy and numeracy skills within a business context. In addition, many of the tasks aim to develop digital literacy and skills for life and work.

Outcomes and experiences

The selected topics also target learning that will ensure learners develop skills and knowledge that will enable them to make informed decisions as they progress to National and Higher pathways. The following outcomes and experiences are extensively covered within the book:

I can explain why a group I have identified might experience inequality and can suggest ways in which this inequality might be addressed.	SOC 3-16a
I can discuss the extent to which my choices and decisions are influenced by the ways in which I am informed.	SOC 3-17b
I can describe how the interdependence of countries affects levels of development, considering the effects on people's lives.	SOC 3-19a
When participating in an enterprise activity, I can explore ethical issues relating to business practice and gain an understanding of how businesses help to satisfy needs.	SOC 3-20a
I can present conclusions about the impact of the globalisation of trade on patterns of work and conditions of employment in Scotland, the UK or beyond.	SOC 3-20b
I can understand the necessity for budgeting and determine ways to manage finance, considering possible investment opportunities, savings, risks or borrowing needs.	SOC 3-21a
I can explore the impact, contribution and use of various software applications and emerging hardware in business.	TCH 3-08a

Online support

All tasks are supported by task sheets that can be downloaded from the Bright Red website. In addition, files to support word processing, spreadsheet, database and PowerPoint® tasks can also be found on the Bright Red website.

The book is supplemented by a full, integrated Level 3 Project, which can be downloaded from our website. Learners can apply all the skills and knowledge acquired from the outcomes and experiences in this book to this practical enterprise project, which involves setting up and managing a school radio station. Alternatively, learners can embark on the practical enterprise project and then develop a deeper understanding of the skills and knowledge acquired from the project by completing the outcomes and experiences in the book. Whatever approach is taken the tasks offered will ensure enjoyment, challenge and engagement for all students.

Skills for Life and Work

It is important, in this fast-changing world, that students experience and develop key skills for life and work as part of their learning. This will ensure they can become successful learners, responsible citizens, effective contributors and confident individuals. The table below outlines just some of the skills for life and work that learners will develop by completing the tasks in the book:

Literacy	Numeracy	Problem-solving	Teamwork	Presenting
Researching	Thinking	Analysing	Organising	Independent learning
Digital skills	Creating	Describing	Writing	ICT skills
Explaining	Report writing	Working with others	Listening	Evaluating

Features you will find in this book

CHAPTER TITLE

This highlights the skill(s) that you will cover in a chapter, including the experience and outcome.

What's coming up?

This explains the benchmarks(s) linked with the topic and skills you are learning.

How does that work?

General examples and worked examples which explain methods, strategies and techniques for answering questions and solving the problems in Classroom challenges.

Classroom challenge

This book is filled with Classroom Challenges, a collection of bright and colourful tasks with plenty of examples to build up your knowledge and consolidate your skills.

TEACHING NOTES

A guidance sheet for this task is available on the Bright Red website - www.brightredpublishing.co.uk

Templates, guides and notes can be downloaded entirely free from the Bright Red Publishing website (www.brightredpublishing.co.uk).

Download extra activities from www.brightredpublishing.co.uk

This free bundle collates further material available, extra research you can do and additional tasks, also to be found online on our website.

Finally, you can find useful tips, hints and important information highlighted in our **Don't Forget** pointers.

DON'T FORGET

Ethics is about doing the right thing.

Everything you don't yet know is something that you can learn!

Best of luck getting down to business!

NEEDS AND WANTS, GOODS AND SERVICES

As human beings we all have **needs** and **wants**. People's needs are limited. We need basic items such as food, water, clothing and shelter in order to survive. We also have emotional needs such as security, love and social acceptance.

Businesses satisfy needs and wants in many different ways. A business exists to make money and to do this, they must decide whether to produce **goods** or provide a **service** or both. Individuals then consume these by purchasing or using them. Anyone who uses a good or service is known as a **consumer.**

When participating in an enterprise activity, I can explore ethical issues relating to business practice and gain an understanding of how businesses help to satisfy needs.

SOC 3-20a

What's coming up?

In this unit of work, you will learn about:

- what is meant by needs and wants
- how organisations help satisfy our needs and wants
- ethical issues relating to business practice
- how ethical issues impact upon organisations.

To be successful with this unit of work you should:

- complete activities
- develop key skills in decision making, organisation and team working
- develop literacy, numeracy and digital literacy skills
- participate in class/group discussions
- provide your teacher with evidence of all the work that you have undertaken.

NEEDS AND WANTS

As human beings we all have **needs** and **wants**. People's needs are limited. We need basic items such as food, water, clothing and shelter in order to survive. We also have emotional needs such as security, love and social acceptance.

Together with the oxygen in the air, we are able to stay alive with these items but without them, we would not be able to survive. After these basic needs have been satisfied, people often then start to desire more. These desires are called wants and are a luxury that we would like to have, but without it, we would be able to survive.

Wants can be unlimited. We constantly want things which will, in our opinion, improve our quality of life and make us feel happier. We can all say that we want the latest iPhone or want another pair of trainers, but we do not need these things in order to live so these would be a 'want' rather than a 'need'.

Classroom challenge

TASK 1 - Creative Thinking - Paired Activity

Make a short list of need and want items that you personally have or would like. Then discuss with a partner, are there any similarities?

TEACHING NOTES

A guidance sheet for this task is available on the Bright Red website - www.brightredpublishing.co.uk

TASK 2 - Problem Solving - Identifier - Solo Activity

Look at each item listed below. Tick the correct box to identify if it is a need or a want.

Item	Need	Want
Water		
Designer handbag		
Car		
Clothes		
Secure place to live		
Sweets		
Luxury cruise		
Heating (within your home)		
Timberland boots		
Fitbit		
Torch		
Jeans		
Basic food (for example, bread)		
Laptop		
Television		

TEACHING NOTES

A guidance sheet for this task is available on the Bright Red website - www.brightredpublishing.co.uk

TASK 3 - Problem Solving - Word Search - Solo Activity

Find the following words in the word search below.

Need Sweets Mobile
Food Computer
Bread House
Water Trainers
Holiday Car Clothes

N	B	Y	A	D	I	L	O	H
S	R	E	N	I	A	R	T	W
N	E	V	N	A	P	L	H	Y
I	T	S	E	H	T	O	L	C
X	U	H	M	D	U	H	P	R
S	P	C	A	S	G	F	Z	P
W	M	J	E	S	S	O	R	B
E	O	L	Y	U	F	E	X	R
E	C	D	T	I	T	O	O	E
T	R	A	C	A	N	W	O	A
S	O	Z	W	S	D	T	D	D
J	A	U	A	Y	O	E	F	C
M	O	B	I	L	E	E	E	I
N	C	L	E	M	L	A	V	N

TEACHING NOTES

A guidance sheet for this task is available on the Bright Red website - www.brightredpublishing.co.uk

TASK 4 - Problem Solving - Unscrambler - Solo Activity

Unscramble the following words and write them out correctly.

Scrambled	Correct version	Scrambled	Correct version
Susienessb		uxylru	
Uevrivs		sipretenre	
Dinmulite		trwae	
cibsa tiesm		diftassie	
Gyxone		oyhalid	
Odfo		lhtsere	
Denes		lebimo	

TEACHING NOTES

A guidance sheet for this task is available on the Bright Red website - www.brightredpublishing.co.uk

TASK 5 - Creative Thinking - Discussion - Paired Activity

Discuss the following with a partner. Why do you think the three items listed below are needs and not wants?

- Drinking water
- Warm clothing
- Sheltered, secure place to live

Write your thoughts down in your workbook and share with the rest of the class.

NEEDS AND WANTS IN SOCIETY

Wants are often an upgraded version of something we need. Just think how many different versions of the iPhone there have been and will continue to be!

DON'T FORGET

Through advertising and clever marketing, we are made to believe that each version is better than the last and that we really NEED to buy one.

Nowadays, there is an ever-increasing desire for wants such as luxury holidays, the latest gadgets and mobile phones to be satisfied. However, as time has passed and technology has improved some items which were once thought of as 'wants' have now become 'needs' in today's society. These include items such as dishwashers, central heating and televisions.

Classroom challenge

TASK 6 - Literacy - Quick Questions - Solo Activity

Answer the following questions in full sentences in your workbook.

1. Explain the difference between a need and a want.
2. Explain why you think dishwashers and central heating are now seen to be a need.
3. State two more examples of items which may once have been labelled a want but are now seen as a need.
4. Outline what would happen if you spent all your money on wants rather than needs.
5. Describe how you think that your wants would be different if you lived in a developing country.
6. In your opinion, does the amount of money we have impact on the choices we make regarding our needs? Explain your answer.
7. Outline the needs you should consider purchasing before buying a want item.

TASK 7 - Problem Solving - Paired Activity

On a sheet of paper, copy out the diagram below. Use as much of the page space as possible. Discuss with a partner where you think each of the following items will fit on the diagram, that is, whether you think it is a need or a want.

A bed Guitar Watch Cuddly toy Rice

Toys Mobile phone Money Toothpaste Water

Clothes Vitamins Candle House Medicine

Blankets Takeaway pizza Laptop

Warm winter coat Pencil

Bike Crisps Bread Books Torch

DON'T FORGET

To make things more complicated, just because something appears to be a need doesn't necessarily mean that it is. For example, a takeaway burger is food but not a need as it is a luxury item and there are cheaper, healthier alternatives available to us.

Choosing Needs and Wants in Society

Every day we all have to make choices. Choices over which clothes to wear, what to eat for breakfast, which perfume or aftershave to wear, which jacket to put on, how much money to take, what to have for dinner, what television show to watch, what homework to do first – the list can be endless. However, we don't have endless amounts of money or time when making these decisions.

When we go to the shops, we may want to buy lots of things – new jeans, new boots, a new bag, another gadget – but we can't. We must consider our choices very carefully and consider each option. We want to use the limited amount of money that we have sensibly and ensure that we get the most value or satisfaction from spending our money.

Classroom challenge

TASK 8 - Creative Thinking - Solo Activity

You have £40 in your purse or wallet but you know you will not get any more money for another week. Make a list of eight items in your workbook that you would choose to buy which you think are essential for the next week.

TASK 9 - Literacy - Creative Thinking - Group Activity

Using the template below, discuss your choices from Task 8, in particular your top four items, with three other classmates. Complete the table below with the necessary information. Remember to include your own choices.

Person's Name	First Choice	Second Choice	Third Choice	Fourth Choice

Are your choices different? Or are there any similarities?

Why do you think this is? Write your thoughts in your workbook.

TEACHING NOTES

A guidance sheet for this task is available on the Bright Red website - www.brightredpublishing.co.uk

TASK 10 - Literacy - Problem Solving - Solo Activity

Look at the list of options to choose in the table below. Which would you choose to maximise your satisfaction? Why? Complete the table with your detailed responses.

Options	Choice	Explain your choice
1. Going to the cinema **or** 2. doing your homework		
1. Eating sweets **or** 2. eating a bag of chips		
1. A holiday in Spain **or** 2. a second-hand motorbike		
1. A new t-shirt **or** 2. a donation to charity		

TEACHING NOTES

A guidance sheet for this task is available on the Bright Red website - www.brightredpublishing.co.uk

TASK 11 - Creative Thinking - Discussion - Paired Activity

Imagine that you are to be sent to a deserted island in a tropical area for a year. You are given a list of possible items that you can take. But...

You can only take ten of these:

Matches Axe Saucepan
Knife Suntan lotion Deodorant
Blanket Jar of hard-boiled sweets Tent
Dog Water-purifying tablets Rope
Guitar Insect repellent Radio
Cuddly toy Camera Torch
Magnifying glass Toilet paper
Two bottles of water
Small tin of black paint Box of chocolates
Spare pair of socks

Discuss with a partner which items you will take and put them into order of importance from 1 to 10. Are all of the items you chose needs and are they essential?

TEACHING NOTES

A guidance sheet for this task is available on the Bright Red website - www.brightredpublishing.co.uk

DON'T FORGET

Different people have different needs and wants depending on their lives, personalities and experiences!

HOW BUSINESSES SATISFY NEEDS AND WANTS

Businesses satisfy needs and wants in many different ways. A business exists to make money and, to do this, it must decide whether to produce **goods** or provide a **service** or both. Individuals then consume these by purchasing or using them. Anyone who uses a good or service is known as a **consumer.**

Goods are items that are **tangible**, which means they can be seen and touched.

How does that work?

Examples include:

Chocolate

Toys

Cars

Juice

Classroom challenge

TASK 12 - Creative Thinking - Solo Activity

Make a list of the items classed as goods which you have used so far today in your workbook. Share these with the class.

TASK 13 - Digital Literacy - Problem Solving – Solo Activity

Go online and research goods which are produced in the UK. For example, you may wish to look at Irn Bru or goods produced by Tunnocks.

Create a short PowerPoint presentation. You should include details about the items you have found such as location of production, price and description of the products and any other relevant information. Try to find at least four products. You should present your information in no more than five slides. Use appropriate formatting, graphics and animation to enhance your presentation.

Save your presentation as PP1. You may now wish to present your finds to your class.

Services are items that are **intangible**, which means they cannot be seen or touched by us. Businesses provide services which do something for us and then we as consumers buy them.

How does that work?

Examples include:

Car Valet

Haircut

Cinema Trip

Banking

Classroom challenge

TASK 14 - Creative Thinking - Solo Activity

Make a list in your workbook of the items classed as services which you have used in the last ten days. Share these with the class.

TASK 15 - Problem Solving - Identifier - Solo Activity

Read each item and tick the correct box to identify if it is a good or a service.

Item	Good	Service
Irn Bru		
Laptop		
Dry cleaners		
Clothes		
4K Television		
Sweets		
Education		
Firefighter		
Luxury cruise		
House insurance		
Banking		
Train journey		
Cheeseburger		
Haircut		
Paperclip		
Make-up		

Item	Good	Service
Shoelaces		
Trip to a museum		
Pencil		
Pizza delivery		
Internet banking		
Jeans		
Cake		
Massage		
Mobile phone		
Paddling pool		
Sandwich		
Petrol		
Toothbrush		
Trip to the cinema		
Skateboard		
Taking a flight to Mexico		

TEACHING NOTES

A guidance sheet for this task is available on the Bright Red website - www.brightredpublishing.co.uk

Download extra activities from www.brightredpublishing.co.uk

Classroom challenge

TASK 16 - Digital Literacy - Problem Solving – Solo Activity

Choose any two businesses you are familiar with and design a poster using software of your choice showing the goods and services provided by each business.

Ensure your poster makes use of different formatting styles, images, colour, a page border if you wish and any other enhancement to ensure your poster is eye-catching.

TASK 17 - Creative Thinking - Solo Activity

Imagine it is now 30 years in the future, what might your needs and wants be now? To satisfy these needs and wants, what goods and services do you think might now exist? Note these down in your workbook.

TASK 18 - Digital Literacy - Solo Activity

Visit the following websites online and, in your workbook, list some of the goods and services provided by each business.

www.superdry.com
www.johnlewis.co.uk

Goods and services can be **durable**, which means they are long lasting and can be used over and over, such as clothes, cars or internet banking. They can also be **non-durable**, which means that they are used up quickly and may only be used once, such as a sandwich, a can of Irn Bru or a holiday. Once these items have been enjoyed, they no longer exist unless the consumer buys another one.

Classroom challenge

TASK 19 - Problem Solving - Identifier - Solo Activity

Read each item and tick the correct box to identify if it is durable or non-durable.

Item	Durable	Non-durable
Cappuccino		
PC		
Holiday to Florida		
Jacket		
Textbook		
Chewing gum		
Education		
Cutlery		
Perfume		
Trip to the cinema		
Shower gel		
Manicure		
Shoes		
Candle		

DON'T FORGET

Goods and services are produced to satisfy our ever changing needs and wants!

How does that work?

Let's look at Literacy – keywords

Keyword	Definition
Need	A good or service that is required because it is essential to survive
Wants	These are goods or services that are not essential but we desire or wish for them
Goods	These are materials or items which are purchased to satisfy human needs and wants. These are tangible objects, that is, can be touched and could be food, computers or clothes
Services	These are actions that a person does for someone else. These are intangible, that is, cannot be touched and could be a haircut, medical check-up or banking
Durable	Goods/services that are long lasting and can be used again and again
Non-durable	Goods/services that only last a short period of time and, in some cases, are only able to be used once
Consumer	Someone who uses a good or a service
Tangible	Goods that **can** be seen or touched
Intangible	Services that **cannot** be seen or touched

AN ETHICAL APPROACH

Ethics are moral guidelines that tell us if what we are doing is right or wrong. They are the values and principles which influence how we behave towards society. We know it is wrong to steal from someone because this could end up in people being hurt as a result of our actions.

DON'T FORGET

Ethics is about doing the right thing.

Before doing anything, we need to consider the following:

- **Impact** – Who will the decision affect or harm?
- **Fairness** – Will my decision be considered fair by those affected?

Businesses need to consider these factors too. **Business ethics** are the values and principles which influence the business world and how businesses behave. We, as consumers, expect that businesses are honest and try to operate responsibly in a manner that will not impact negatively on society. We trust them to produce goods and services that meet our needs and wants and that do not cause harm to any other person or the environment.

A big business has a lot of power, which it can either use responsibly or selfishly. Many firms operate to meet the needs and demands of their owners and do not consider the needs of their employees, customers or the local community in which they operate. However, not all businesses behave or operate in a socially responsible manner. Dumping waste products is one example of an unethical and illegal practice by a business.

Other business owners believe that acting ethically increases costs and so reduces profits. Paying below average wages lowers the firm's total costs, which for many is too attractive a prospect, but society sees this as being greedy. A business can also cut costs by hiring child labour at very low wages in developing countries but this is completely unethical.

An ethical business will carefully consider the implications of what they are doing and the effect it might have on the community and the environment. Having a **social responsibility** allows businesses to 'give something back' to the community, improve their image and reputation and correct the **social costs** which may have been caused by the business and its operations.

Social costs are the negative effects upon a local community that are caused as a direct result of a new business. These could include additional air, water or noise pollution, or extra congestion on the roads.

Social benefits are good things which happen to a local community as a result of a new local business. This could be improved roads, a new bus route, additional housing or the creation of jobs for members of the community.

A business with a reputation for being socially responsible will attract consumers who are happier buying from a business that operates ethically. It could also attract potential employees who identify with the aims of the business.

Classroom challenge

TASK 20 - Creative Thinking - Thought Shower

Visit the *About us* sections online for Marks & Spencer, Sainsbury's and Tesco.

In your workbook write down ways which each of these businesses demonstrate that they are trying to behave in an ethical manner. For example, you may wish to find out how they treat employees, how they contribute positively to the environment and how they demonstrate that they are environmentally friendly.

BUSINESSES BEHAVING ETHICALLY

There are many decisions to be made by businesses but sometimes these decisions have an ethical side to them.

Characteristics of an Ethical Business

How does that work?

Here are some ethical decisions that businesses have to make:

- We have had some reports of a product we produce being harmful to the health of consumers, has it been removed from the market?
- Do we offer the same rights to all our staff, even temporary members?
- Do we offer a good work/life balance to our staff?
- Do we offer regular training opportunities to all staff?
- Are health and safety procedures in place to protect our employees?
- Have we ensured that disabled access and toilet facilities are available?
- Are we paying the correct wages to all our employees?
- Have we removed any excessive packaging from our goods or have we managed to use packaging that has been recycled and is recyclable?

If a business can answer yes to these questions, then it could be described as operating ethically.

Classroom challenge

TASK 21 - Digital Literacy - Solo Activity

Click the link on our website to watch the video and answer the questions.

1. What are Mr Burns and Smithers doing in the park when they get caught?
2. What is different about the squirrel?
3. What is the name of the Agency who catch Mr Burns and Smithers in the act?

Creative Thinking - Paired Activity

For each of the following paired goods, suggest whether you think each good is a **need** or a **want**, clearly stating why. You may feel that is not an easy or clear-cut decision to make. Once you have discussed each pair of goods with your partner, record your thoughts in your workbook as to which good is a need and which good is a want.

Cereal vs Bread Mobile phone vs Facebook Coca Cola vs Tap water

Classroom challenge

TASK 22 - Digital Literacy - Researching - Solo Activity

Go online and search for companies that have built up a reputation for acting unethically, either in the past or currently. Choose one company and type up a brief report in Word outlining the unethical issues you have discovered, for you to send to the company's Head Office as an unhappy customer. You could suggest alternative actions that you feel would be more ethical and acceptable to society.

ADVERTISING A ENTREPRENEU

Businesses use advertising in order to inform the consumer about the goods or services they sell. A business may sell the best product on the market but if consumers do not know about it then they most likely will not buy it.

An **entrepreneur** is someone who:

- comes up with a good idea for a business – perhaps 'spots a gap in the market'
- organises all the elements or resources needed for the business to work
- takes a risk by putting money and time into the business.

AD
VER
TIS
ING

I can discuss the extent to which my choices and decisions are influenced by the ways in which I am informed. SOC 3-17b

What's coming up?

Learning Intentions

In this unit of work, you will learn about:

- the role of advertising
- the role and importance of logos and straplines to help consumers make informed choices
- the way in which businesses use advertising to influence consumers' choices and decisions
- the qualities of successful entrepreneurs and find out how they use advertising to inform, persuade and remind consumers of their goods and services.

Success Criteria

To be successful with this unit of work you should:

- complete activities
- develop literacy, numeracy and digital literacy skills
- participate in class/group discussions
- provide your teacher with evidence of all the work that you have undertaken.

THE ROLE OF ADVERTISING

Businesses use advertising in order to inform the consumer about the goods or services they sell. A business may sell the best product on the market but if consumers do not know about it then they most likely will not buy it. This means a business will not grow and become successful. This is a major reason why businesses spend so much time and money creating advertising campaigns to inform consumers of the benefits of their goods or services.

There are **three** main reasons for advertising:

1. 

When a business wants to **inform** the consumer, for example, about a new good or service they are offering

2. 

When a business wants to **persuade** the consumer to buy their good or service

3. 

When a business wants to **remind** consumers of their good or service

Go to www.brightredpublishing.co.uk and watch the three video clips, which are examples of advertisements trying to inform, persuade and remind the consumer of a good or service.

METHODS OF ADVERTISING

Businesses use different methods to advertise their goods and services to the consumer.

Method	Advantage	Disadvantage
Television – many businesses advertise on television during breaks between programmes	Your business can reach a wide audience over a large geographical area	It is expensive to advertise on television
Radio – many businesses advertise during radio programmes	Your business can reach a wide audience and it is cheaper to advertise on the radio than it is on television	The consumer cannot see the goods being advertised
Cinema – many businesses show advertisements before a blockbuster film starts!	It is a captive audience – they cannot change the channel!!	It is very expensive to advertise in the cinema
Social Media – many businesses have their own social media account such as a Facebook page	Many people all over the world have access to social media on their smartphones, tablets or computers	Some social media sites allow customers to leave comments that could be negative. This can harm the reputation of the business
Billboards/Posters – many businesses put up posters/billboards in places where they think lots of consumers will be	Consumers will see the advertisement every time they pass by the location	The posters or billboards could be vandalised and so would not look very good
Newspapers – many businesses place an advert in national and local newspapers	Consumers will usually take their time to read newspapers so are more likely to see advertisements	Adverts in newspapers are usually printed in black and white so the advertisement is not as appealing
Magazines – many businesses place adverts in magazines such as gossip, fashion or lifestyle magazines	Adverts can be printed on glossy paper and in colour so look very eye-catching to consumers	Advertising in magazines only targets a group of like-minded people

HOW EFFECTIVE IS ADVERTISING?

Advertising, using the methods described in the table above, can be very effective when trying to persuade consumers to buy a good or service.

Classroom challenge

TASK 1 - Paired Activity

In the table below are three advertisements of some very popular and well-known products. Your task is to identify the message that the advertisement is highlighting. Write the answers in your workbook.

1

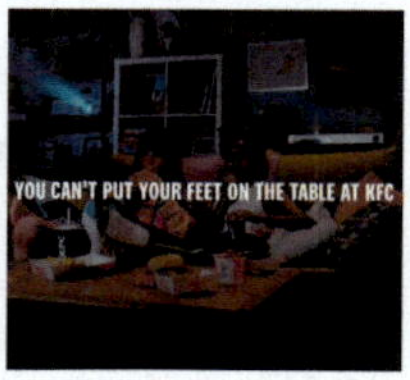

2

3

TEACHING NOTES

A worksheet for completing this task is available on the Bright Red website - www.brightredpublishing.co.uk

We will now have a look at examples of advertising that can be seen on television, cinema and online using social media sites such as Facebook, Instagram and other social media.

How does that work?

Go online to the Bright Red website and click to watch the three videos listed there.

For each of the three videos:

1. Identify the **good** or **service** being advertised.
2. Write down the message that each advertisement is highlighting about the good or service.

Write your answers in your workbook.

CHOICES

We live in a world where money is not unlimited and that is especially true when we are talking about our own personal finances. We therefore cannot buy everything we would like to. Businesses know that we have to make informed choices on how we spend our limited income. Many businesses use a logo to enable consumers to quickly identify their product from those of their competitors.

What is a logo?

A logo is a symbol that is made up of text and an image or graphic that helps us identify well-known brands of goods and services. A business will spend time and money creating a logo so that it will be memorable and attractive to the consumer.

Classroom challenge

TASK 2 - Solo Activity

Ask your teacher for the Task 2 worksheet – **Identifying Famous Logos**

Identify the name of the business or product from each of the logos shown below.

TEACHING NOT

A guidance sheet for this task is available on the Bright Red website - www.brightredpublishing.co.u

Straplines

In additional to creating a logo, the business will create a catchy saying or slogan that they hope the consumer will easily remember and associate with the good or brand of the business. Some straplines have been so successful that they have made it into everyday conversation!

How does that work?

An example of such a successful strapline is:

McDonald's – i'm lovin it

DON'T FORGET

Good straplines will tell the consumer the best thing about the good and/or the business. It will become an important part of the business's image.

i'm lovin' it®

Classroom challenge

TASK 3 - Solo Activity

Below is a list of well-known straplines. In your workbook write down the name of the organisation or good that is being referred to:

1	Just do it	
2	Because I'm worth it	
3	Every little helps	
4	Finger lickin' good	
5	The ultimate driving machine	
6	Eat Fresh	
7	Snap! Crackle! Pop!	
8	Taste the Rainbow	
9	Have a break	
10	Once you pop you just can't stop	
11	The World's Local Bank	
12	The Make-up of Make-up Artists	

TEACHING NOTES

A worksheet for completing this task is available on the Bright Red website - www.brightredpublishing.co.uk

Packaging - How Does This Encourage the Consumer to Buy Goods?

Businesses use eye-catching packaging so that their goods will stand out on supermarket shelves. Businesses spend a great deal of time and money deciding on the design of their good's packaging.

Why?

The main reasons are:

- the business wants the good to look as attractive as possible
- to provide information
- to protect the good

And finally, they hope that this will encourage the consumer to buy the good.

How does that work?

Here are some examples of goods packaging that you may know.

Classroom challenge

TASK 4 - Solo Activity

You are the Marketing Manager of a confectionery business called Chocalot and you are introducing a new chocolate snack bar.

This chocolate bar is low in fat (only 99 calories per bar), has a rich chocolate taste and provides a good source of energy and vitamins. The company wish to market the new chocolate bar specifically to young people aged 14–18 years old.

The company want this chocolate bar to be seen as a healthy alternative to other chocolate bars without compromising on taste and quality – this is what makes the new chocolate bar so unique.

You need:

- Computer
- Coloured pens/pencils
- Glue stick
- Ruler
- Scissors
- Paper

Using the wrapper template, design the wrapper for your new chocolate bar. **Ask your teacher for the wrapper template sheet.**

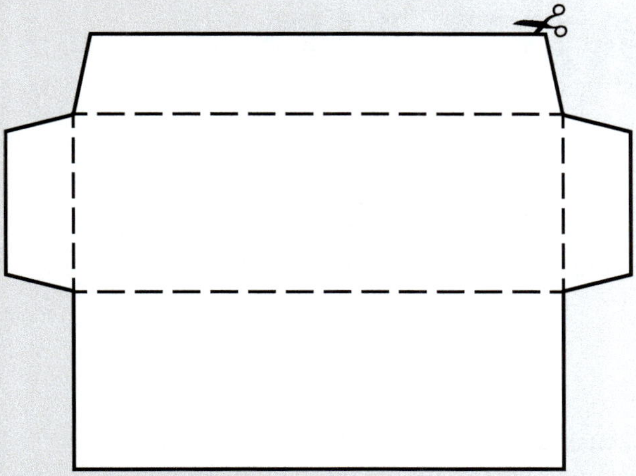

Chocolate Wrapper Template
Print the wrapper template.
Cut out the wrapper template.
Score and fold on the dashed line.
Glue the flaps

Remember to include on your wrapper the following:

- The name of your chocolate bar
- A barcode (you could source an image of a barcode online)
- A logo
- A strapline
- Company name
- 99 calories

TEACHING NOTES

A wrapper template can be downloaded from the Bright Red website (www.brightredpublishing.co.uk, where you can also find an additional packaging design task.

THE ROLE OF ENTREPRENEURS

An **entrepreneur** is someone who:

- comes up with a good idea for a business – perhaps 'spots a gap in the market'
- organises all the elements or resources needed for the business to work
- takes a risk by putting money and time into the business.

There is no qualification for being an entrepreneur. In many cases, successful entrepreneurs have no formal qualifications – but they do have to have drive, ambition and vision. You may be familiar with the successful entrepreneurs listed below.

Arnold Clark – car sales

Sir Charles Dunstone – mobile phone retailer

Sir Richard Branson – airlines, cosmetics, trains, media

Sir James Dyson – electrical appliances, including vacuum cleaners

Simon Cowell – entertainment/television/music

Sir Alan Sugar – technology/electronics

Mark Zuckerberg – social media

Archie Hewlett – designer shoes (fans include Tinie Tempah and Justin Timberlake)

What are the Personal Qualities of An Entrepreneur?

The entrepreneurs above are likely to share common characteristics and it is these characteristics that have made them so successful and their products a household name.

Classroom challenge

TASK 5 - Solo Activity

If we look at the list of entrepreneurs on the previous page, what personal qualities do these business people have to make them so successful? What characteristics of their personality drives them to achieve this great success? Write as many as you can think of in your workbook.

TASK 6 - Solo Activity - Research and Presentation Task

Instructions:

Choose two entrepreneurs you are keen to learn about. You may choose two of the entrepreneurs from the previous page. Go online and research some basic information on your chosen entrepreneurs.

Find out:

- the business name
- the type of business – what do they make or sell?
- what age they were when they started their business
- how much profit their business made last year
- how these businesses advertise their goods or services, for example, on television.

Present your findings, on the two entrepreneurs, using presentation software. Include a suitable design template and pictures of the company products and/or logo to make your presentation attractive to your audience. Print one copy of the presentation, ensuring your name is displayed in the page footer.

BILLBOARDS AND POSTERS

Businesses often use billboards and posters to advertise their goods and services. If you are in a car or walking along the street you will often see large billboards advertising products or services. They are usually displayed in places where lots of cars or people will be passing by so that the maximum number of people can see the advertisement. You may also find posters on the side of bus shelters, in underground stations or pasted onto street walls.

A business may also hand out leaflets on the street or post them through the letterboxes of people's homes. This means people can read the information on the leaflet at a time that suits them.

Classroom challenge

TASK 7 - Solo Activity - CASE STUDY

Read the case study below and then complete the tasks that follow.

Jessica and Kaydi have been in business for one year. The childhood friends first considered the idea of going into business two years ago. They decided to open an indoor skate park facility in a large disused warehouse on the outskirts of their town. There are also outdoor facilities for the summer months. They called the park Skater Island.

In addition, in order to maximise their income, they decided to have a skateboarding accessories shop and a café offering snacks and hot and cold drinks. Their daily opening hours are 10am to 10pm. They have decided to lower the entrance fee to £5 for adults and £3 for children for a two-hour slot in the park.

Jessica and Kaydi are keen that as many people know about the park and what it offers so that they can attract as many customers as possible. This will ensure that the park is successful and makes a good profit. Jessica thinks that they should post a leaflet through the letterbox of local residents.

Part A

In your workbook, write down six important pieces of information that should be included in the leaflet. Hint – read the case study again!

Part B

You work in the office of the skateboarding park. Jessica has asked you to design the leaflet that was mentioned in the case study. Please ensure you include the information that you listed in Part A.

DON'T FORGET

The purpose of the leaflet is to inform customers about the skate park and to persuade people to use the park and spend as much money as possible.

You need:

- Computer
- Coloured pens/pencils
- Glue stick
- Ruler
- Scissors
- Paper

You could also design your leaflet by using word processing or desktop publishing software.

Classroom challenge

TASK 8 - Problem Solving - Word Search and Unscrambler - Solo Activity

Ask your teacher for the worksheets to tackle the task below or go online to the Bright Red website to download them there. Unscramble the words to uncover some keywords learned in this unit.

ristvdngaie	
lrsntiape	
ogod	
loog	
rsonumec	
sreecvi	

TEACHING NOTES

Worksheets for this activity can be found on the Bright Red website - www.brightredpublishing.co.uk

Find the following words in the word search below:

ADVERTISEMENT	**BILLBOARD**	**CINEMA**	**CONSUMER**
ENTREPRENEUR	**GOOD**	**LOGO**	**PACKAGING**
QUALITIES	**SERVICE**	**STRAPLINE**	

A	B	G	E	S	L	Q	B	C	R	C	Z	I	S	S
T	I	I	L	N	E	P	O	L	Q	I	V	S	T	E
R	B	O	K	S	T	R	Y	X	I	N	Y	F	R	I
H	G	W	J	B	M	R	V	E	A	E	S	B	A	T
O	J	B	Z	L	V	X	E	I	V	M	X	S	P	I
V	X	N	P	L	N	L	Q	P	C	A	X	S	L	L
D	R	A	O	B	L	L	I	B	R	E	S	G	I	A
A	D	V	E	R	T	I	S	E	M	E	N	T	N	U
U	W	Q	U	J	D	G	V	Q	G	I	N	G	E	Q
D	O	O	G	Z	B	N	A	Y	G	K	E	E	I	S
I	T	Q	W	D	Z	E	P	A	U	P	D	R	U	C
N	X	V	K	M	V	F	K	E	M	Z	N	E	Y	R
L	Q	O	X	P	L	C	O	N	S	U	M	E	R	N
G	W	V	B	T	A	L	F	W	S	O	X	T	K	X
C	A	J	B	P	V	I	D	S	I	T	G	L	S	V

TEACHING NOTES

Teacher's notes for this activity can be found on the Bright Red website, where this wordsearch can be downloaded.

EQUALITY AND DISCRIMINATIO

When we leave school, most of us will find a job in order to earn money to pay for our **needs** and **wants** in life. When we have searched and found a job we want to do, in order to pay for these **needs** and **wants**, it is important that we are all treated equally.

UK legislation to protect people from being discriminated against is called the Equality Act 2010. It seeks to protect people from discrimination on the grounds of age, disability, race and sex.

"I can explain why a group I have identified might experience inequality and can suggest ways in which this inequality might be addressed." SOC 3-16a

What's coming up?

Learning Intentions

In this unit of work, you will learn about:

- what is meant by inequality
- situations which demonstrate inequality
- laws which exist to promote equality in the workplace and society
- how employers try to ensure equality in the workplace.

Success Criteria

To be successful with this unit of work you should:

- complete activities
- develop literacy, numeracy and digital literacy skills
- participate in class/group discussions
- provide your teacher with evidence of all the work that you have undertaken.

WORKING AS EQUALS - WHAT DOES THIS MEAN?

When we leave school most of us will find a job in order to earn money to pay for all our **needs** and **wants** in life. **Needs** are things that we need to survive such as shelter, food and clothing, but we also have **wants** such as cars, holidays and technology like games consoles and mobile phones.

When we have searched and found a job we want to do, in order to pay for these **needs** and **wants,** it is important that we are all treated equally in the following areas:

When applying for a job in an organisation.

Whilst working for or being employed in that organisation.

Why do organisations need to make sure that we are all treated equally?

It is the law!

This means that organisations must not treat people differently to others or they may be prosecuted under these laws and face fines, as well as gaining a bad reputation for breaking these laws.

Classroom challenge

TASK 1 - Creative Thinking - Paired Activity

With a partner try to think of differences between people or characteristics people may have that may mean they are treated differently or unequally compared with others. Write your thoughts down in your workbook. The first one is given to help you.

1. Age	5.
2.	6.
3.	7.
4.	8.

TEACHING NOTES

A worksheet for this task can be downloaded from our website www.brightredpublishing.co.uk

THE LAW ON EQUALITY OR EQUALITY LEGISLATION

The UK Parliament introduced this **legislation** to protect people from being treated differently in all parts of their life and not just work. However, for the purposes of this unit, we are going to focus on employers and how they need to follow the Equality Legislation.

The name of this legislation is the Equality Act 2010.

Download the Homework Helper file from www.brightredpublishing.co.uk for a short video explaining the purpose of the Equality Act 2010

Classroom challenge

TASK 2 - Solo Activity

Go online to the Bright Red website and watch a short video explaining the purpose of the Equality Act 2010

TASK 3 - Solo Activity

Log onto your computer and access the Equality Act 2010 legislation using the link on the Bright Red website.

Complete the table below in your workbook writing down the eight **protected characteristics** listed in the legislation.

1.	**5.**
2.	**6.**
3.	**7.**
4.	**8.**

FOCUSING ON FOUR OF THE PROTECTED CHARACTERISTICS

We are now going to look at in more detail the unequal treatment of or **discrimination** against individuals in employment because of their:

- Race
- Sex
- Age
- Disability

Race Discrimination

Organisations must be careful that they do not act in a way that prevents equal treatment of employees or potential new employees of all races and ethnicities.

DON'T FORGET

According to the **Equality Act 2010** as mentioned above, there should be no discrimination when people are of different *'races including colour, nationality, ethnic or national origin'.*

How does that work?

Watch the short video clip using the link on the Bright Red website. Answer the questions below in your workbook by watching and listening carefully. You can stop and/or replay the video so you can find the answers and write them down.

1. State the number of CVs that the Sheffield researchers sent out.
2. Identify the three names put on the top of the CVs.
3. State three types of people that recruiters are likely to 'sift' or remove.
4. The video says there are types of people we are 'hard-wired' to like. Identify these types of people.
5. Outline what may happen if we keep making these unconscious decisions when recruiting employees.

Developing Literacy Skills.

Copy and complete the table below in your workbook.

Word in video clip	Meaning
unconscious	
CV	
objective	

DON'T FORGET

You may not know the meaning of some of the words listed in the table. Access an online dictionary to find out their meaning. If it helps you can write the meaning beside the word in the table.

Sex Discrimination

Organisations must be very careful not to treat people unequally based on their sex or gender. **The Equality Act 2010** says that the Act continues to protect all genders against discrimination on the grounds of their sex, for example, paying women less than men for doing the same job.

How does that work?

You can watch a short video clip on the Bright Red website for further explanation. Answer the questions in your workbook by watching and listening carefully. You can stop and/or replay the video so you can find the answers and write them down.

TEACHING NOTES

This worksheet can be completed electronically by downloading a copy from the Bright Red website – www.brightredpublishing.co.uk

1. Describe what the manager does when the woman gives her answer to reducing the waste in the organisation.
2. Outline what the manager continues to do every time the female employee suggests something during the meeting.
3. Identify the kind of feelings the female employee may experience during the meeting.
4. Outline advice you would give to the manager so that he could manage the meeting better.

Age Discrimination

The Act protects employees of all ages so that they are not treated unfairly because of their age. However, there are certain jobs where employers could say that a person of a certain age would not be able to physically do the job.

Classroom challenge

TASK 4

Can you think of any jobs where being, for example, aged 90, would not be suitable?

Write your answer(s) in your workbook.

How does that work?

You can watch a short video clip on the Bright Red website for further explanation. Answer the questions in your workbook by watching and listening carefully. You can stop and/or replay the video so you can find the answers and write them down.

1. Identify one stereotype of young people that was mentioned in the video.
2. Identify one stereotype of older people that was mentioned in the video.
3. Is it easier for companies to cover a single day absence or long-term absences?
   Explain your answer.
4. State two things that can happen to workers when they get to their late 40s in age.

DON'T FORGET

You may not know the meaning of some of the words listed in the table. Access an online dictionary to find out their meaning. If it helps you can write the meaning beside the word in the table.

Developing Literacy Skills.

Copy and complete the table below in your workbook.

Word in video clip	Meaning
stereotype	
absence	

TEACHING NOTES

This worksheet can be completed electronically by downloading a copy from the Bright Red website – www.brightredpublishing.co.uk

Disability Discrimination

The Equality Act 2010 says that you must not be discriminated against because you have a disability which is either a physical disability or a mental disability. This means you should be treated the same as others who do not have a disability.

For example, during an interview, a job applicant tells the potential employer that he has multiple sclerosis. The employer decides not to appoint him even though he's the best candidate they have interviewed, because they assume he will need a lot of time off sick.

This is **discrimination**! The potential employer is not going to employ this person because they have this illness. The only reason for not employing a particular person is that there is someone else who they think can do the job better.

Classroom challenge

TASK 5

Can you think of any jobs where having a physical disability may make a person not suitable for a job because of the physical requirements of the job?

How does that work?

You can watch a short video clip on the Bright Red website for further explanation. Answer the questions below in your workbook by watching and listening carefully. You can stop and/or replay the video so you can find the answer and write it down.

1. Identify the two main types of disability.
2. Outline what is meant by 'discrimination by association'.
3. Identify the responsibility the employer has for staff with a disability.
4. State two actions employers should not do to staff with a disability.
5. Outline the situation detailed in the video where employers can legally discriminate.

What can employers do to support people with disabilities?

How does that work?

You can watch a short video clip on the Bright Red website for further explanation. Answer the questions below by watching and listening carefully. You can stop and/or replay the video so you can find the answers and write them down.

1. Identify the piece of equipment Rita said she needed to make her job easier.
2. Explain what is meant by 'Assistive Technology'.
3. Describe the training the company gave to the other employees so they could understand Amir's needs.

Classroom challenge

TASK 6 - Solo Activity - Case Study

Read the case study below.

Joe has suffered from osteoarthritis, which means he has a lot of pain in the joints in his hip. He has had this pain for the last three years. Joe is currently employed as a Personal Trainer at 'Go Gym' fitness club and has worked with them for the past ten years. Joe finds that if he stands for too long then the pain gets worse. He thinks working full time is too tiring, because of the pain.

In your workbook, can you think of two changes to Joe's job that 'Go Gym' could agree to so that Joe is able to earn a living and continue to work for the fitness club?

DISCRIMINATION – PEOPLE APPLYING FOR JOBS

Organisations must follow the **Equality Act 2010** and not have rules and procedures that allow for discrimination when trying to recruit and select people for jobs within their organisation. We are first of all going to look at the first step used by an organisation when trying to recruit or employ staff for a job – **THE JOB ADVERTISEMENT.** These can be found in:

Newspapers

Magazines

Job Websites

Government jobcentres known as Jobcentre Plus

Classroom challenge

TASK 7 - Solo Activity

Look at the two job advertisements shown below and write down the words used in the job advert that you think are promoting inequality in terms of **race**, **sex**, **age** or **disability**.

Explain how these words could be seen to be discriminatory.

Write your answers in your workbook.

Job Advertisement 1

Busy city centre law firm is looking for an Assistant Manageress to manage the day-to-day activities of the office.

Duties include:

- Production of reports
- Accounts Management
- Payroll
- Supervising staff
- Database Management

Only people born in the UK should apply and as the job is very demanding then no applications of people over 50 will be accepted.

To apply send an email to:

andersonsolicitors@yahaa.com

Job Advertisement 2

Hamilton House Builders

Working Site Foreman

Duties include:

- Managing and co-ordinating the on-site workmen
- Report progress to Site Manager
- Keep daily records of project progress and updating the phase one document
- Physical work so people with physical disabilities should not apply, especially those in a wheelchair

Personal Qualities Required:

- Male applicants preferred as mainly a male workforce
- Non-citizens of the UK should not apply
- Applicants must be aged between 18 to 35.

Email: JobsHHB@yahaa.co.uk to apply.

TASK 8 - Solo Activity - Creative Task

Create an information leaflet on the four characteristics that we have previously worked through. Include the following pieces of information:

- Full name of the equality legislation
- The names of the four characteristics we have talked about in this chapter
- A description of what discrimination of each of these characteristics means.

Also, when creating your information leaflet:

- Use appropriate graphics
- Use a variety of fonts
- Insert a page border
- Use different text formatting such as bold, italic and underlining.

Make your information leaflet as eye-catching as possible!

TASK 9 - Solo Activity - Problem Solving

Complete the Equality Act 2010 word search.

C	H	A	R	A	C	T	E	R	I	S	T	I	C	S	L	T	E	E	G
T	E	F	D	V	H	F	E	C	P	G	Q	Q	F	E	B	P	Q	P	E
Z	Q	I	L	Y	O	V	N	K	A	U	H	P	G	K	I	A	O	L	N
R	B	O	D	O	I	P	M	A	J	R	G	I	T	S	W	B	Q	R	D
D	T	Q	L	T	T	Y	S	K	Q	M	S	U	G	W	M	C	T	Y	E
N	I	T	I	K	U	R	D	A	P	L	D	J	T	R	A	L	L	T	R
U	C	S	N	O	I	T	C	A	A	I	T	E	B	P	C	E	F	I	K
A	O	G	C	G	K	C	S	T	D	A	B	X	T	R	U	X	A	L	P
P	M	S	I	R	E	U	I	Y	I	K	I	R	U	C	Q	N	A	A	N
Q	G	P	N	S	I	O	Q	K	S	Z	W	B	V	S	E	X	M	U	E
I	M	I	S	I	N	M	R	U	A	L	I	G	T	P	S	T	M	Q	G
G	F	E	R	C	K	P	I	L	D	T	P	L	V	F	W	B	O	E	A
Z	W	S	M	F	Z	C	H	N	V	Z	H	Y	I	R	R	D	L	R	M
T	M	U	Y	T	I	L	I	B	A	S	I	D	Q	E	B	O	Y	I	P
W	A	F	T	G	D	D	H	X	N	T	L	L	U	D	T	S	G	E	B
B	G	F	D	P	O	P	A	Z	T	R	I	G	H	T	S	H	P	J	M
J	A	K	U	T	J	F	A	F	A	O	D	O	C	V	U	P	N	M	L
S	S	U	A	V	A	A	A	C	G	T	M	B	N	W	X	T	A	I	Y
D	Y	B	C	H	E	N	O	T	E	Z	Z	B	E	L	R	Z	N	G	C
W	T	J	G	I	A	R	D	K	Y	W	I	A	S	W	I	D	P	A	Z

ACCESS
ACT
ACTION
AGE
CHARACTERISTICS
DISABILITY
DISADVANTAGE
DISCRIMINATION

EQUALITY
ETHNIC
GENDER
LEGISLATION
POSITIVE
PROTECTED
RACE
RIGHTS

TEACHING NOTES

A worksheet can be downloaded for completion of this task from the Bright Red website - www.brightredpublishing.co.uk

How does that work?

Let's look at Literacy – Keywords

Keyword	Definition
Need	A good or service that is required because it is essential to survive. For example - food, clothing and shelter
Wants	These are goods or services that are not essential but we desire or wish for them. For example - mobile phones, games consoles
Legislation	A law or set of laws suggested by a government and made official by a parliament
Equality	The state of being equal, especially in status, rights and opportunities
Discrimination	Unfair treatment of people based on, for example, age, race, religion or disability
Ethnic	A social group that shares a common and distinctive culture, religion or language

BUDGETING AND MONEY

Individuals must manage the money they receive and spend. When individuals **spend** more than their **income**, they are likely to build up **debt**. Entrepreneurs must also manage money flowing in and out of their business. This process of money management is called budgeting.

Managing money is a very important skill for everyone and you will find out about different ways to do this in this unit.

I can understand the necessity for budgeting and determine ways to manage finance, considering possible investment opportunities, savings, risks or borrowing needs.
SOC 3-21a

What's coming up?

Learning Intentions
In this unit of work, you will learn about:

- the importance of budgeting for individuals and small business organisations
- the preparation of budgets
- the importance of saving for the future
- how to calculate interest on savings
- different borrowing options including hire purchase
- the risks associated with borrowing.

Success Criteria
To be successful with this unit of work you should:

- complete activities
- participate in class/group discussions
- provide your teacher with evidence of all the work that you have undertaken.

INTRODUCTION TO BUDGETING

Individuals must manage the money they receive and spend. When individuals **spend** more than their **income**, they are likely to build up **debt**. Entrepreneurs must also manage money flowing in and out of their business. When a business has insufficient money flowing in, they may be unable to pay their outgoings such as wages, electricity and their suppliers. As a result, there is a chance they could be declared **bankrupt**.

Individuals and **businesses** must plan ahead and prepare a cash budget.

- A cash budget is usually prepared for either a week, a month, several months or a year.
- A cash budget details all items of cash received and paid.
- A cash budget will have an **opening balance** and a **closing balance**.

CASH BUDGETS FOR INDIVIDUALS

Layout of a Cash Budget for an Individual

How does that work?

An example of the layout of a cash budget for an individual is shown below.

Cash Budget for **John Smith**
For week ending **20 January 2023**

	£	£
Opening Balance		X
RECEIPTS (Cash In)		
Wages	X	
Loan	X	
Cash gift	X	
		X
PAYMENTS (Cash Out)		
Clothes	X	
Food	X	
Train fares	X	
Cinema	X	X
Closing Balance		X

A Worked Example

Cash Budget for **Sean Devine**
For Week ending **20 January 2023**

	£	£
Opening Balance		50
RECEIPTS (Cash In)		
Wages from paper round	20	
Loan	10	
Gift from father	12	42
		92
PAYMENTS (Cash Out)		
Youth club weekly fees	5	
Lunch costs	20	
Train fares	14	
Cinema	8	47
Closing Balance		45

DON'T FORGET

The Closing Balance for one week/month will become the Opening Balance for the next week/month.

PRACTICAL EXERCISES - CASH BUDGETS FOR INDIVIDUALS

Complete the following tasks in your workbook.

Classroom challenge

TASK 1

Prepare the Cash Budget for Vikki Taylor – Week 1

	£
Opening Balance	40
Pocket money	10
Swimming	5
Lunch	8
Purchase of new shirt	12
Cinema	9
Train fares	4
Loan from Mum	6
Wages from Saturday job	25

TASK 2

Prepare the Cash Budget for Sean Devine – Week 1

	£
Opening Balance	35
Wages	30
Cash gift from sister	26
Youth club fees	10
Purchase of books	15
Mobile phone bill	10
Lunch	8
Ticket for football match	12

TASK 3

Prepare the Cash Budget for Sandra Grant – Week 1

	£
Opening Balance	40
Wages	30
Theatre	20
Weekly train fares	12
Book	5
Lunch with friend	10
New school bag	15
Loan from brother	15

TASK 4

Prepare the Cash Budget of Lesley McCallum for Weeks 1 and 2.

Week 1	£	Week 2	£
Opening Balance	95	Opening Balance	?
Wages	80	Wages	80
Badminton fees	12	Overtime earnings	20
Housekeeping payment to Mum	20	New shirt	14
Celebrity magazines	8	Housekeeping payment to Mum	20
Repairs to mobile phone	20	Theatre	22
Dinner with friends	12	Repaid part of loan to Dad	10
Cinema	8	Mobile phone bill	15
Purchase of T-shirt	10		
Loan from Dad	16		

TASK 5

Prepare the Cash Budget of Sean Cahill for Weeks 1 and 2.

Week 1	£	Week 2	£
Opening Balance	200	Opening Balance	?
Loan from Gran	65	Wages from Saturday job	40
Wages from Saturday job	40	Lunch with brother	10
Train fares	12	New T-shirt	12
Purchase of books	10	Mobile phone bill	15
Cash gift from sister	60	Repaid part of loan to Gran	25
Dinner with friend	16	Train fares	8
Birthday present for brother	12		
Mobile phone top-up	15		

DON'T FORGET

The closing balance from week 1 becomes the opening balance for week 2.

TASK 6

Prepare the Cash Budget of Rachel Young for Weeks 1 and 2.

Week 1	£	Week 2	£
Opening Balance	45.00	Opening Balance	?
New shoes	40.00	Repaid part of loan to Mum	40.00
Loan from Mum	100.00	Wages from part-time job	65.00
Dinner and cinema with friend	35.00	Mobile phone bill	20.00
Birthday present from brother	10.00	Magazines	6.50
Cash gift from sister	20.00	Sale of watch	36.00
Wages from part-time job	65.00	Train fares	12.75

TEACHING NOTES

Download a template for this task at www.brightredpublishing.co.uk

At the end of **Week 2**, Rachel is thinking of buying a second-hand iPad from a friend. They have agreed a price of £150. Can Rachel afford to make this purchase?

CASH BUDGETS FOR BUSINESSES

It is not only individuals who use Cash Budgets to plan their expenditure – businesses need to budget too. They need to have enough money to pay all their bills – including wages. It may be necessary to arrange an overdraft or a loan from the bank to pay bills or buy new assets if they are likely to incur cash flow problems.

Layout of a Cash Budget for a Small Business

How does that work?

An example of the layout of a cash budget for a small business is shown below.

Cash Budget for Martin's Newsagents for June–August 2023

	£ **June**	£ **July**	£ **August**
Opening Balance	X	X	X
RECEIPTS (Cash In)			
Cash Sales	X	X	X
Loan	X		
	X	X	X
PAYMENTS (Cash Out)			
Wages	X	X	X
Gas	X	X	X
Electricity	X	X	X
Rent and Rates	X	X	X
	X	X	X
Closing Balance	X	X	X

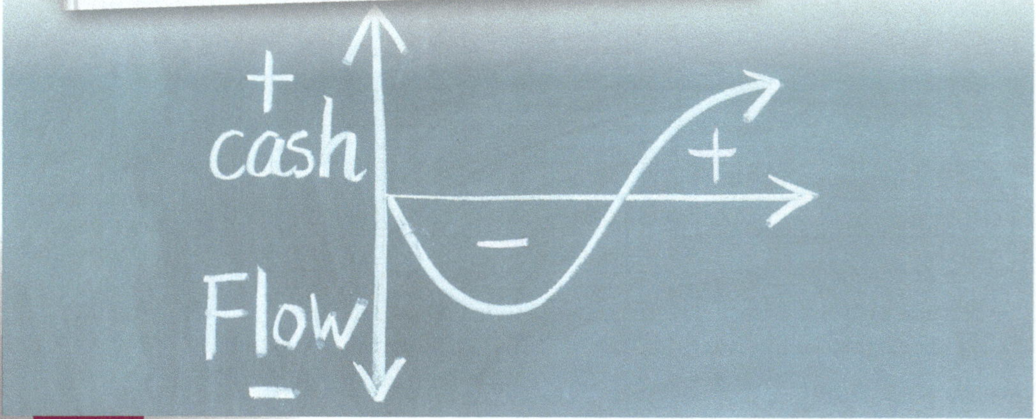

A worked example

LIAM DONNELLY
CASH BUDGET FOR PERIOD JUNE AND JULY 2023

	June	July
	£	£
Opening Balance	5,000	6,350
Receipts		
Cash Sales Revenue	1,950	4,100
Loan	2,000	
	3,950	4,100
Payments		
Cash Purchases	1,500	2,400
Wages	400	400
Rent and Rates	150	150
Advertising	50	150
Purchase of Equipment	500	
	2,600	3,100
Closing Balance	6,350	7,350

Practical exercises - cash budgets for small businesses

Classroom challenge

TASK 7

Mahira Fareed has set up a small coffee shop called 'Coffee Beans'. Here are her forecast receipts and payments for August and September 2023

Bank at 1 August	£6,000
Cash Sales	August £3,300 September £6,100
Cash purchases	August £1,700 September £2,000
Wages of employees	£550 per month
Rent and Rates	£250 each month
Advertising	£75 per month
Computer	A computer will be purchased in August at a cost of £2,000: this will be paid in four equal instalments from August to November
Electricity	£100 per month
Cleaning	£25 per month

Using the above information, prepare the cash budget of Coffee Beans for August and September.

DON'T FORGET

The closing balance for August will become the opening balance for September.

TASK 8

Alexis Rose has set up a small newsagents called 'The News Stand'. The following are her forecast receipts and payments for June and July 2023

Bank Balance at 1 June	£7,000
Cash Sales	June £3,500 July £5,000
Cash purchases	June £2,000 July £1,800
Wages	£160 for each employee per month – there are two employees
Rent and Rates	£250 per month
Advertising	£300 per month
Equipment	Equipment will be purchased in June at a cost of £1,200: this will be paid in three equal instalments in June, July and August
Electricity costs	£35 per month
Grant	A government grant of £1,800 will be received in June

Using the above information, prepare the cash budget of The News Stand for June and July.

DON'T FORGET

The closing balance for June will become the opening balance for July.

Advantages of Preparing a Cash Budget

Preparing a Cash Budget can:

- help an individual to plan their spending for the coming weeks or months
- highlight areas where an individual is overspending
- assist an individual to save regular amounts of money each week to purchase expensive items like a computer or iPad.
- reduce the risk of overspending and accumulating debt.

Classroom challenge

TASK 9

Christopher Boyle has set up a fast-food business called 'The Burger Joint'. The following are his forecast receipts and payments for October–December 2023

Opening Balance at 1 October £1,500

Sales – October £700, November £450, December £520

Purchases – October £620, November £800, December £820

Wages - £250 per month

Rent and Rates - £50 per month

Gas and Electricity- £40 per month

Equipment costing £600 will be purchased in October. This will be paid for in three equal instalments in October, November and December

Advertising: £50 per month

Christopher will receive a government grant of £500 in December

Using the above information, prepare the cash budget of The Burger Joint for October–December.

DON'T FORGET

The closing balance for October will become the opening balance for November. The closing balance for November will become the opening balance for December.

DIGITAL LITERACY

What is a spreadsheet?

A spreadsheet is a computer application program that enables the user to present numerical information and perform calculations using formulae. A spreadsheet comprises a grid of 'cells' arranged in rows and columns and information can be inserted into each cell.

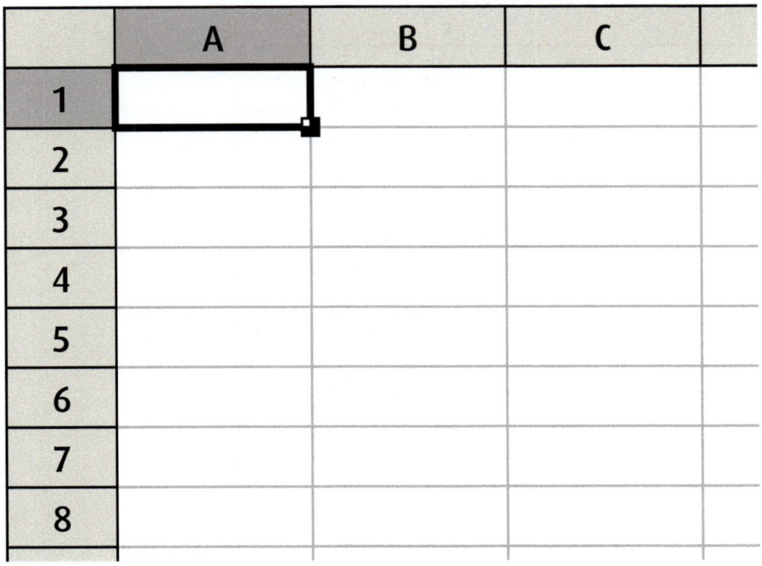

Each cell can contain text, numbers and formulae. A formula is a calculation based on the contents of cells. The total in that formula can change if the content of cells is changed. Spreadsheets can be useful for preparing budgets.

How does that work?

Look at the examples shown below.

EXAMPLE 1

	A	B	C	D
1	**Cash Budget for Vikki Taylor – Week 1**			
2				
3			£	£
4	**Opening Balance**			40
5				
6	**Receipts**			
7	Pocket money		10	
8	Loan from Mum		6	
9	Saturday job		25	=Sum(C7:C9)
10				=D4+D9
11	**Payments**			
12	Swimming		5	
13	Lunch		8	
14	New shirt		12	
15	Cinema		9	
16	Train fares		4	=Sum(C12:C16)
17				
18	**Closing Balance**			=D10-D16

EXAMPLE 2

	A	B	C	D	E
1	**Cash Budget for Liam Donnelly – June and July 2023**				
2			£	£	
3			**June**	**July**	
4	**Opening Balance**		5,000	=C18	
5					
6	**Receipts**				
7	Cash Sales Revenue		1,950	4,100	
8	Loan		2,000		
9			=sum(C7:C8)	=sum(D7:D8)	
10					
11	**Payments**				
12	Cash Purchases		1,500	2,400	
13	Wages		400	400	
14	Rent and Rates		150	150	
15	Advertising		50	150	
16	Purchase of Equipment		500		
17			=sum(C12:C16)	=sum(D12:D16)	
18	**Closing Balance**		=(C4+C9)-C17	=(D4+D9)-D17	

Study the formulae highlighted above. These are standard formulae used for preparing a cash budget.

DON'T FORGET

Once formulae have been entered into the cells, the totals will automatically update if the amount of any receipt or payment changes.

Classroom challenge

TASK 10

Instructions

1. You should complete Tasks 1–9 again using spreadsheet software.
2. You can prepare the spreadsheets yourself or you can use a template available to download from the Bright Red website.
3. Insert your name in a footer and print one copy of each task.

SAVINGS, BANK ACCOUNTS AND INTEREST RATES

Today there is a lot of pressure on people to save money. If you have enough to pay for everything you need, why should you worry about putting money aside each month? There are a variety of reasons for saving money. Different people save for different reasons.

Classroom challenge

TASK 11

Working with your partner, or in a group, try to identify four good reasons why it is important that people try to save some money every week/month.

Write these in your workbook.

TYPES OF BANK ACCOUNT

Current Account

Most people have a **CURRENT ACCOUNT** with a bank or building society to manage their money.

A current account allows you to:

- Receive your salary, pension or benefits to be paid directly into your bank.
- Pay bills such as electricity or mortgage payments directly from your bank.
- Pay for shopping using a debit card rather than carrying large amounts of cash or having to access cashpoint machines.
- Withdraw cash from cashpoint machines when banks are closed.
- Arrange an overdraft (a type of short-term loan) from the bank when you are temporarily short of cash or overspend.

Savings Account

Savings accounts can be a great way of putting away money for a special purchase or as a 'nest egg' for the future. A savings account is intended to store money over a long period. This can be useful when saving up for something special like a deposit for a house, a car or a holiday or simply to ensure you have money available in case of an emergency.

There are two main types of Savings Account

EASY ACCESS SAVINGS ACCOUNT	NOTICE SAVINGS ACCOUNT
You can add or withdraw from your savings account whenever you like.	You usually cannot access your money for perhaps one or two years.
Interest rates are usually quite low.	Interest rates are usually higher.

DON'T FORGET

The main attraction of a savings account is that you earn interest on your savings - you can even earn interest on your interest!

CALCULATING INTEREST

When you put money into a bank account and agree to leave your money in the account for a set period of time, the bank will reward you with interest at the end of the year.

How does that work?

If Christopher Boyle deposited £200 into the bank on 1 January 2023 and agreed to leave this money in the bank until 31 December 2023 (one full year) the bank will reward him with 2% interest. How much money will Christopher then have at the end of the year?

Answer

£200 × 2% = £4. Christopher will get back the original £200 he deposited plus £4 interest. In total, he will be worth £204 at the end of the year.

Developing Numeracy Skills

Classroom challenge

TASK 12

Complete the table below in your workbook by calculating the amount of interest that each customer will receive from the bank at the end of the year. You should also show the total value of savings for each customer after interest has been added.

TEACHING NOTES

Download a template for this task at www.brightredpublishing.co.uk

Name	Savings Deposited	Interest Rate	Annual Interest Earned	Total Value of Savings
J Smith	£100	2%		
C Kelly	£600	2%		
L Hamilton	£500	2.5%		
H Loudon	£1,000	2%		
C Blake	£200	2.5%		
N McPhee	£2,000	5%		
K Clark	£1,500	2%		
L Spears	£400	4%		

DIGITAL LITERACY

How does that work?

Task 12 can also be completed using spreadsheet software. Create the following spreadsheet (or access the spreadsheet file already created and replace the letter 'f' in columns D and E with appropriate formulae).

	A	B	C	D	E
1	Name	Savings Deposited	Interest Rate	Interest Earned	Total Value of Savings
2	J Smith	£100	2%	f	f
3	C Kelly	£600	2%	f	f
4	L Hamilton	£500	2.5%	f	f
5	H Loudon	£1,000	2%	f	f
6	C Blake	£200	2.5%	f	f
7	N McPhee	£2,000	5%	f	f
8	K Clark	£1,500	2%	f	f
9	L Spears	£400	4%	f	f

Consider using the following formulae:

=B2*C2

=B2+D2

Classroom challenge

TASK 13

The Bank of Scotland offers an interest rate of 2% per annum (per year) on savings.

How much interest would you receive on the following amounts of money at the end of one full year?

(a) £600 (b) £1,400 (c) £500 (d) £1,000

Advantages of saving

- Saving provides financial security for the future.
- Large items of expenditure, like purchasing a holiday, can be financed without the need for borrowing.
- Interest is earned. The more money you save the more interest you receive.

Disadvantages of saving

- Goods and services cannot be purchased when money is being saved.
- Interest rates may be very low and so the rewards for saving are not great.

Classroom challenge

TASK 14 - Comparing Different Savings Accounts

Go online to visit the websites shown below and select a savings account offered by each bank. Complete the table below in your workbook by writing a short description of the account and the current interest rate offered.

TEACHING NOTES

This table can be downloaded from the Bright Red website www.brightredpublishing.co.uk

Bank	Description of Savings Account	Interest Rate
www.bankofscotland.co.uk 		
www.rbs.co.uk 		
www.santander.co.uk Santander		

If you were to invest £1,000 in each of the accounts you have described above, how much interest would be earned in each account if the money was invested for one full year?

Write your answer in your workbook.

BORROWING MONEY

Why do people borrow money?

People borrow money for several reasons:

- To purchase assets such as houses or cars. Purchasing these products requires large amounts of money that people may not have, so borrowing becomes a must.
- To undertake diy projects such as installing a new kitchen or bathroom.
- To pay for an expensive holiday.
- To pay off other loans that are due for repayment.
- To cover the difference between a person's income (wages) and their expenditure. Some people live beyond their means and must borrow to finance the difference.

TYPES OF LOAN

Mortgage	This is a loan used to buy property. It is a long-term loan and is usually repaid over a long period, for example, 25 years.
Personal Loan	This is used to pay for goods such as cars, furniture or to pay for a holiday.
Credit Card	The card can be used to purchase goods and services on credit (up to an agreed amount). When you start to repay the amount spent on the card, you are then able to start purchasing more goods and services.

Calculating Interest on a Personal Loan

If a bank decides to give you a loan, they will require you to pay interest in addition to the amount you have borrowed. This can make borrowing money expensive. Loan repayments are usually made monthly and will include a charge for interest.

How does that work?

Example 1

Patrick Roach borrows £10,000 at an interest rate of 5% to be repaid over one year in 12 monthly repayments. Calculate each monthly repayment.

Step 1 £10,000 × 5% = £500

Step 2 £10,000 + £500 = £10,500

Step 3 £10,500/12 months = £875 per month

Developing Numeracy Skills

Example 2

Scott McGimpsey takes a personal loan of £1,600 at a rate of 5% per annum simple interest to be repaid over one year.

Calculate the **total** amount to be repaid and the **monthly** repayment. Note this in your workbook.

Example 3

Jane Peckham takes a personal loan of £1,200 at a rate of 2% per annum simple interest to be repaid over one year.

Calculate the **total** amount to be repaid and the **monthly** repayment. Note this in your workbook.

Example 4

Mike Corbett takes a personal loan of £10,000 at a rate of 2% per annum simple interest to be repaid over one year.

Calculate the **total** amount to be repaid and the **monthly** repayment. Note this in your workbook.

Advantages of Personal Loans

- You can choose how long you would like to take to repay the loan.
- Loan repayments will usually be a fixed amount each month, which makes it easier to budget.

Disadvantages of Personal Loans

- Personal loans usually carry high rates of interest.
- Most banks will not usually lend less than £1,000 so you may borrow more than you need.

Classroom challenge

TASK 15

Eddie Carroll has recently opened his own hairdressing salon. He has decided to apply for a bank loan of £5,000 to purchase equipment for his salon. He would like to repay the loan and interest over 48 months (four years). He has asked you to use the websites shown in the table on page 65 to calculate the monthly repayments and the total amount that will be repaid over the four-year period.

Write your answers in your workbook.

Advise Eddie which bank you would recommend he take a personal loan with.

TEACHING NOTES

The table shown for Task 14 can be re-used from page 65

HIRE PURCHASE

What is Hire Purchase?

Hire purchase is when a business allows customers to purchase goods and pay for them in instalments over an agreed period of time. Because the customer is not paying for the goods in cash at the point of sale, interest is added to the cost of the product. This makes the product more expensive.

How does that work?

Example 1

Kirsty Heung wishes to buy a second-hand car with a price tag of £5,000 for her son on hire purchase.

The Hire Purchase Agreement states the following:

- Deposit required: £1,000
- Repayment amount: £150 per month
- Number of repayments: 36

You are required to calculate the difference between the cash price and the price paid on hire purchase at the end of the three-year agreement.

Solution

By buying the car on hire purchase

£1,000 + (36 × £150) = £6,400

Kirsty is paying an additional £1,400

£6,400 – £5,000 = £1,400

Developing Numeracy Skills

Complete the following tasks in your workbook.

Classroom challenge

TASK 16

Lucie Natche is planning on entering a hire purchase agreement to install a new kitchen in her home. If she was paying in cash, the total cost would be £6,500.

The Hire Purchase Agreement states the following:

- Deposit required: £1,200
- Repayment amount: £120 per month
- Number of repayments: 48

You are required to calculate the difference between the cash price and the price paid on hire purchase at the end of the four-year agreement.

TASK 17

Willie Njupsa is planning on entering a hire purchase agreement for the purchase on a new computer. If she was paying in cash, the total cost would be £500.

The Hire Purchase Agreement states the following:

- Deposit required: £0
- Repayment amount: £30 per month
- Number of repayments: 24

You are required to calculate the difference between the cash price and the price paid on hire purchase at the end of the two-year agreement.

TEACHING NOTES

These templates can be downloaded from www.brightredpublishing.co.uk

Advantages of Hire Purchase

- Deposits are small and sometimes no deposit is required at all.
- The cost of the purchase is spread over several months.
- The customer has access to the product immediately.

Disadvantages of Hire Purchase

- Interest is added to the cost of the product making it more expensive.
- The customer does not own the product until the final payment is made – the seller has the right to take the product back if the customer fails to make payment.

DEVELOPING LITERACY SKILLS

Classroom challenge

TASK 18

Find the following words in the Word Search below.

Income	Debt	Bankrupt
Opening Balance	Closing Balance	Receipts
Payments	Cash Budget	Spreadsheet
Cell	Formula	Saving
Interest Rate	Current Account	Savings Account
Loan	Hire Purchase	

E	G	H	I	N	C	O	M	E	H	G	J	K	L	P	O
J	N	J	J	L	O	H	L	I	P	O	T	R	V	A	W
H	I	R	E	P	U	R	C	H	A	S	E	S	S	Y	S
J	Q	R	H	T	Y	K	O	I	Y	J	K	L	H	M	K
J	J	D	E	B	T	K	L	O	P	J	T	U	T	E	J
J	K	L	O	O	O	L	I	K	I	M	L	O	P	N	I
C	S	A	V	I	N	G	S	A	C	C	O	U	N	T	B
L	K	Y	U	Y	I	K	U	J	K	I	B	M	I	S	A
O	P	E	N	I	N	G	B	A	L	A	N	C	E	D	N
K	J	K	M	N	K	I	U	N	H	K	U	E	J	K	K
I	H	J	K	T	K	I	L	O	P	O	P	L	J	K	R
N	J	Y	U	E	I	O	M	K	M	P	K	L	J	U	U
G	I	J	K	R	E	C	E	I	P	T	S	L	K	O	P
B	M	H	J	E	J	I	L	I	O	Q	U	Y	T	F	T
A	K	L	O	S	J	K	L	O	O	I	H	J	M	O	S
L	S	S	S	T	B	N	J	L	O	A	N	K	U	R	I
A	J	K	U	R	K	I	U	J	J	U	N	M	J	M	B
N	N	M	J	A	H	J	K	I	N	Y	Y	L	O	U	P
C	N	Y	J	T	J	S	A	V	I	N	G	S	H	L	K
E	H	N	U	E	K	I	L	O	P	T	T	Y	E	A	B
C	A	S	H	B	U	D	G	E	T	N	K	L	I	W	V
N	H	K	U	J	U	J	H	T	R	N	J	L	I	Y	L
K	Y	U	I	O	P	P	M	J	Y	U	U	Y	T	K	U
C	U	R	R	E	N	T	A	C	C	O	U	N	T	D	D

TEACHING NOTES

The word-search template can be downloaded from www.brightredpublishing.co.uk

Extension Task

TASK 19

Throughout this unit of work, you have been introduced to many new words and terminology. Working with a partner or in a group, discuss the meaning of the words listed below. Write each word below in your workbook and a short sentence to explain what each word means.

Income	Debt	Bankrupt
Opening Balance	Closing Balance	Receipts
Payments	Cash Budget	Spreadsheet
Cell	Formula	Saving
Interest Rate	Current Account	Savings Account
Loan	Hire Purchase	

1. Prepare the Cash Budget of Haider for Weeks 1 and 2.

Week 1	£	**Week 2**	£
Opening balance	25.00	Opening Balance	?
New shirt	50.00	Repaid part of loan to Dad	35.00
Loan from Dad	90.00	Wages from part-time job	55.00
Dinner with friend	18.00	Mobile phone top-up	25.00
Gift from aunt	12.00	Magazines	7.50
Sold golf club	20.00	Sold DVDs	28.00
Wages from part-time job	55.00	Bus fares	14.75

At the end of **Week 2**, Haider is thinking of buying a second-hand lap-top from a friend. They have agreed a price of £150. Can Haider afford to make this purchase?

2. State one reason why people save money.
3. State one advantage and one disadvantage of saving money.
4. Haider takes a personal loan of £1,200 at a rate of 5% per annum simple interest to be repaid over one year. Calculate the **total** amount to be repaid and the **monthly** repayment.
5. State one advantage and one disadvantage of borrowing money.
6. Outline what is meant by hire purchase.
7. State one advantage and one disadvantage of hire purchase.

GLOBALISATION AND INTERNATIONAL TRADE

Globalisation is the term used to describe the fact that countries are increasingly working together and becoming more dependent on each other. Globalisation has resulted in an increase in the production of goods and services across the world.

Countries buy and sell the goods and services they produce around the world in a process known as international trade. This process has a number of steps, which we will look at in this unit.

UNIT 5: GLOBALISATION AND INTERNATIONAL TRADE

I can describe how the interdependence of countries affects levels of development, considering the effects on people's lives. SOC 3-19a

Having considered responses to a recent international crisis, I can contribute to a discussion of the effectiveness of the responses. SOC 3-19b

What's coming up?

Learning Intentions

In this unit of work, you will learn about:

- globalisation
- reasons for importing/exporting goods and services
- advantages and disadvantages of international trade and specialisation
- Fairtrade
- balancing trade
- exchange rates
- non-governmental organisations (UNICEF, United Nations, etc.)
- how non-governmental organisations respond to a crisis
- the impact of interdependence and globalisation on the lives of UK citizens.

Success Criteria

To be successful with this unit of work you should:

- complete activities
- develop literacy, numeracy and digital literacy skills
- participate in class/group discussions
- provide your teacher with evidence of all the work that you have undertaken.

GLOBALISATION

What is globalisation?

Globalisation is the term used to describe the fact that countries are increasingly working together and becoming more dependent on each other. Globalisation has resulted in an increase in the production of goods and services across the world and an increase in trade (exchanging of goods and services) between countries.

DON'T FORGET

Globalisation refers to closer working relationships between countries across the world.

DON'T FORGET

Multinational organisations have branches across the world.

Most large companies are multinational organisations with branches all over the world, for example, McDonald's, Starbucks and Apple. Globalisation has been taking place for many years, but has recently speeded up. Globalisation has resulted in:

- increased international trade
- a large company operating in more than one company
- countries working together and becoming more dependent on each other.

Global brands are brands that are recognised throughout much of the world. An example of a global brand is shown below:

Google

DON'T FORGET

A global brand is one that is recognised across the world.

Classroom challenge

TASK 1

You should work in a small group of three or four and you may wish to use the internet to help you with this task. Make a list of as many global brands as you can think of. Record your answers in your workbook. Set out your answers as follows:

NAME OF ORGANISATION	GOOD OR SERVICE PROVIDED
McDonald's	Food

TASK 2

Copy the table below into your workbook. Look at the items listed in the first column. For each product, write down the first brand name you can think of.

PRODUCT	BRAND NAME
Mobile phone	
Instant coffee	
Trainers	
Computer game	
Fast food	
Baked beans	
Tissues	
Motor car	

TEACHING NOTES

These templates can be downloaded from www.brightredpublishing.co.uk

INTERNATIONAL TRADE

Countries like the UK **IMPORT** and **EXPORT** many goods and services around the world.

Examples of imported goods

DON'T FORGET

When the UK **imports** products this means that the UK **buys** goods from another country.

Examples of exported goods and services

DON'T FORGET

When the UK **exports** products this means that goods made in the UK are **sold** to other countries in the world.

The UK **imports** goods because:

- There are products that would be difficult to produce in the UK because of the climate, for example fruit.
- Other countries are better (more efficient) at making the product, for example, Japan is more efficient at making motor cars.
- There are certain products that we simply do not have, such as diamonds.

The UK **exports** goods because:

- The UK has some resources that other countries do not have, for example, oil and fresh quality water.
- The UK is more efficient at producing certain products than other countries around the world, for example, whisky and oil.
- The UK must export (sell) goods and services to raise funds to pay for imports.

Because of international trade, countries can **specialise** on what they are good at producing. They are then able to keep what they need for themselves and sell the rest to other countries around the world. This will raise money for these countries to help them purchase goods from other countries that they cannot produce themselves.

Classroom challenge

TASK 3

The table on the right outlines a range of products that are produced by different countries around the world. Complete the country column by writing down the country where each product is made in your workbook. You may wish to use the internet to assist you with this task.

PRODUCT	COUNTRY
Tea	
Coffee	
Whisky	
Chocolate	
Oranges	
Coca Cola	
Wine	
Pasta	
Bacon	
Rice	
Sugar	
Bananas	
Clocks	
Vodka	
Electronics	
Tartan	
Lamb	
Timber	

DON'T FORGET

Most countries around the world will specialise in producing certain goods and services where they have a natural advantage.

Classroom challenge

TASK 4

Answer the following questions in sentences in your workbook.

1. State the meaning of globalisation.
2. Explain the difference between imports and exports.
3. Outline why the UK exports goods and services to other countries.
4. Outline why the UK imports goods and services from other countries.
5. Describe what is meant by the term specialise.

TASK 5 - Developing Digital Literacy

Below are the top ten countries that the **UK EXPORTED** goods to during Year 1.

Create a spreadsheet and enter the data below

Order	Country	Value of Exports (£m)
1	USA	£33,531
2	Germany	£24,760
3	France	£17,871
4	Netherlands	£17,379
5	Irish Republic	£15,295
6	Belgium	£10,456
7	Spain	£8,949
8	Italy	£8,196
9	China	£5,129
10	Sweden	£4,106

Now create a **column chart** like the one shown below.

Put your name in the footer and save the spreadsheet as UK Exports.

Print one copy of your chart.

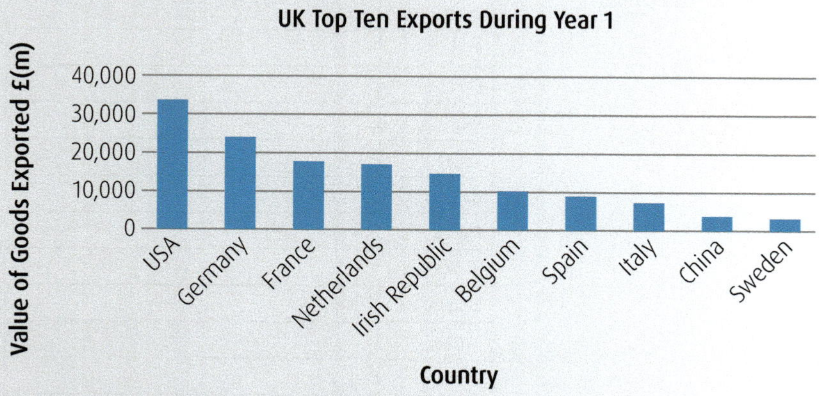

TASK 6

Below are the top ten countries that the **UK IMPORTED** goods from during Year 1.

Create a spreadsheet and enter the data below.

Order	Country	Value of Exports (£m)
1	Germany	£39,131
2	USA	£28,451
3	China	£22,840
4	Netherlands	£21,201
5	France	£20,226
6	Norway	£15,085
7	Belgium	£14,771
8	Irish Republic	£12,218
9	Italy	£11,983
10	Spain	£9,088

Now create a **column chart** like the one shown below.

Put your name in the footer and save the spreadsheet as UK Imports.

Print one copy of your chart.

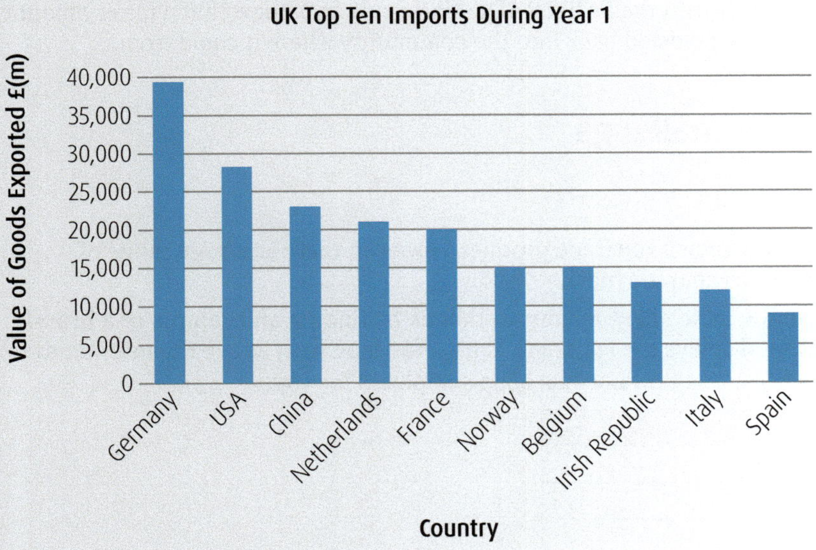

FAIRTRADE

What is Fairtrade?

Fairtrade is a simple yet incredibly important idea – it is all about changing the way trade works so that the people who produce the things you buy get a fairer price for their work. This may seem obvious, but lots of people in low-income countries have to sell their goods at prices so low that they can't make a decent living. Often, only a tiny bit of the money you pay for a product goes to the person who actually made it! This happens a lot when we import products from low-income countries.

Did you know that nearly half the people in the world live on less than £2.00 per day?

How would you feel if you only received a tiny bit of the money you deserved for producing a product you worked hard on? This is where the Fairtrade Foundation comes in.

The Fairtrade Foundation was set up to support producers in low-income countries to get a fairer price for their work. So, when you buy a product with the **FAIRTRADE** Mark on it, you know that a fairer amount of money is being invested back into the community where it came from.

DON'T FORGET

Fairtrade is an attempt to make trade fair so that producers get a better price for the products they produce.

Classroom challenge

TASK 7

Coffee is the most well-known Fairtrade product. However, there is a huge range of products that carry the Fairtrade Mark.

Copy and complete the table below in your workbook by finding an **example of a brand** for each product that displays the Fairtrade Mark. (You may wish to use the internet to help you with this task.) The first one has been completed for you.

Product	Example
Ice cream	Ben and Jerry's
Bananas	
Rice	
Cocoa	
Sugar	
Herbs	
Dried fruit	
Nuts	
Tea	
Fruit juice	
Wine	

TASK 8

Go to the Fairtrade Foundation website – https://www.fairtrade.org.uk/ and select the Buying Fairtrade section.

Using software of your choice, create a poster detailing the products which have been given the Fairtrade mark. Ensure your poster makes use of different formatting styles, images, colour, a page border if you wish and any other enhancement to ensure your poster is eye-catching.

BALANCING TRADE

Balancing trade is an effort to ensure that the value of goods and services **exported** from the UK equals the value of goods and services **imported** into the UK.

However, this does not always happen!

When the UK **exports** more goods than it **imports** it is said to have made a **SURPLUS** on trade.

When the UK **imports** more goods than it **exports** it is said to have made a **DEFICIT** on trade.

Classroom challenge

TASK 9 - Developing Numeracy Skills

For each of the following years, calculate whether the UK has made a surplus or a deficit on world trade. Write your answer in your workbook.

Year 1

UK EXPORTS	UK IMPORTS	SURPLUS/DEFICIT
£(m)	£(m)	£(m)
£175,245	£200,589	

Year 2

UK EXPORTS	UK IMPORTS	SURPLUS/DEFICIT
£(m)	£(m)	£(m)
£182,325	£220,410	

Year 3

UK EXPORTS	UK IMPORTS	SURPLUS/DEFICIT
£(m)	£(m)	£(m)
£192,610	£265,560	

Year 4

UK EXPORTS	UK IMPORTS	SURPLUS/DEFICIT
£(m)	£(m)	£(m)
£205,213	£255,572	

Between **Year 1** and **Year 4**, the UK has **imported** more goods than it has **exported** to the rest of the world.

TEACHING NOTES

These templates can be downloaded from www.brightredpublishing.co.uk

EXCHANGE RATES

When the UK wishes to purchase goods from another country, it has to pay for these goods in the currency of that country. For example, if the UK wishes to purchase goods from the USA it must pay for these in US dollars ($).

The UK must **exchange** pounds sterling (£) for US dollars ($).

Classroom challenge

TASK 10 - Developing Digital Literacy

Copy the table below into your workbook. Go online to research the currency used by the countries shown in the table below.

COUNTRY	CURRENCY
China	
Spain	
Japan	
Bulgaria	
Norway	
Germany	
Sweden	
Ukraine	
Italy	
Canada	

TASK 11 - Developing Numeracy Skills

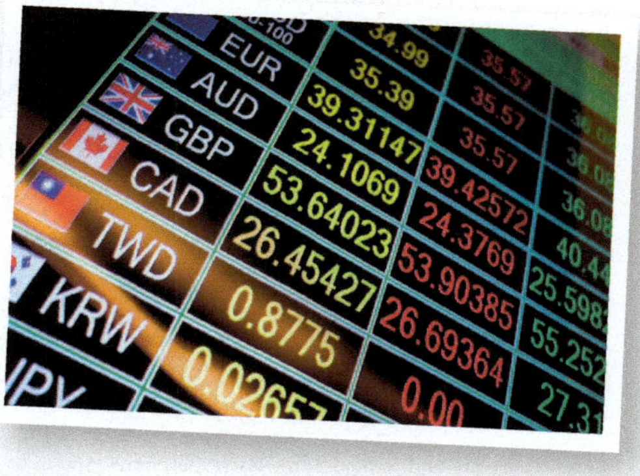

Look at the exchange rates shown below.

£1 =	1·62 US Dollars
£1 =	1·15 Euros
£1 =	1·33 Japanese Yen
£1 =	1·58 Canadian Dollars

Use the currency converter above to answer the following questions in your workbook:

1. Mr Marshall visits the USA and purchases a new jacket for $156 US dollars. How much would this be in UK £ sterling?

2. Mrs Singh will be visiting Japan on a business trip. She is planning on taking £800. How many Japanese Yen will this provide her with?

3. The Semenov family will be going to Spain on a summer holiday. They are planning on taking £1,000 spending money. How many Euros will they have to spend on holiday?

4. While on holiday, the Semenov family intend to dine out for their evening meal. They estimate that this will cost approximately 60 Euros per night. What is the meal costing them in UK £ sterling?

Keywords	Deficit	Euro	International	Surplus
	Currency	Dollar	Trade	
	Exchange Rate	Yen	Specialise	

THE IMPACT OF GLOBALISATION AND INTERNATIONAL TRADE ON THE UK

Positive Impact

Globalisation means that UK citizens have a wider choice of **goods** and **services** in shops and supermarkets. It also means that businesses can sell their products to a much bigger market all over the world and so earn higher **profits**.

International trade helps to keep **prices** in shops low for UK consumers. When businesses are competing with businesses from all over the world, they must be efficient and make sure **prices** are low to encourage consumers to buy from them.

UK businesses can sell their products to other countries like France and Germany. This means they can **expand** and create **jobs** for UK citizens.

Globalisation has resulted in many foreign businesses locating in the UK, for example, Santander, Toyota and Coca Cola. This has meant that many UK citizens now work for foreign employers.

Negative Impact

Many products are made far away that could be made locally, causing unnecessary transportation which is damaging to our environment.

Cultures can be threatened. For example, many local foods may be ignored by consumers who are opting for fast food take aways.

Large companies with a global brand can become too powerful, making it difficult for new entrepreneurs to compete.

Classroom challenge

TASK 12 - Developing Literacy Skills

Find the following words in the word search below:

IMPORTS	TRADE	DOLLAR
YEN	EXPORT	SPECIALISE
DEFICIT	EXCHANGE RATE	BALANCE OF PAYMENTS
EURO	CURRENCY	

I	V	N	M	C	X	H	J	S	S	D	F	B	D	C	K	S
M	T	F	F	H	D	Y	E	R	U	E	X	P	O	R	T	P
P	S	R	D	S	F	D	H	B	R	B	M	J	L	G	D	E
O	D	F	A	D	H	F	D	G	P	K	H	F	L	G	J	C
R	W	E	W	D	D	E	D	S	L	D	F	D	A	F	F	I
T	D	F	D	G	E	U	R	O	U	D	D	S	R	D	S	A
S	I	Y	D	D	F	F	D	F	S	D	F	Y	E	N	H	L
F	Y	H	G	Y	I	E	D	F	G	G	E	D	W	W	E	I
F	H	H	J	H	C	U	R	R	E	N	C	Y	Q	D	D	S
G	J	J	L	H	I	J	U	C	G	V	W	D	E	S	D	E
P	T	G	H	H	T	J	C	V	N	V	E	D	D	D	S	F
E	X	C	H	A	N	G	E	R	A	T	E	D	G	E	P	F
B	A	L	A	N	C	E	O	F	P	A	Y	M	E	N	T	S

TASK 13

Unscramble the following words in your workbook:

USPSLRU ____________________

EDTRA ____________________

YCNERUCR ____________________

TIICFED ____________________

EATR EGANHCXE ____________________

LLODRA ____________________

NEY ____________________

TORPIM ____________________

XORTEP ____________________

OURE ____________________

TASK 14

Answer the following questions in sentences in your workbook.

1. State one reason why the UK imports goods from other countries.
2. State one reason why the UK exports goods to other countries.
3. Select any five countries in the world and state what products they tend to specialise in producing.
4. Identify three countries which the UK exports goods and services to.
5. Identify three countries which the UK imports goods and services from.
6. State when a country would make a surplus on trade.
7. State when a country would make a deficit on trade.
8. Explain the meaning of exchange rate.
9. Identify the currencies of the following countries:
   USA
   Italy
   Japan
   Spain
10. If the exchange rate is $1.55 US dollars to £1 UK sterling how many US dollars would you receive in exchange for £200?
11. Explain how globalisation has had a positive impact on UK citizens.
12. Explain how globalisation may have a negative impact on UK citizens.

NON-GOVERNMENTAL ORGANISATIONS

A non-governmental organisation (NGO) is any non-profit, voluntary citizens' group that is organised on a local, national or international level. NGOs perform a variety of services and humanitarian functions, bringing citizens' concerns to governments. Some are organised around specific issues, such as human rights, the environment or health. They provide expert advice, highlight issues and help to implement international agreements.

DON'T FORGET

A non-governmental organisation is an organisation set up by volunteers and is not concerned with profit.

Examples

ORGANISATION	LOGO	AIMS AND OBJECTIVES
OXFAM		To help create lasting solutions to the injustice of poverty. Oxfam is part of a global movement for change, empowering people to create a future that is secure, just and free from poverty.
SAVE THE CHILDREN		To inspire breakthroughs in the way the world treats children and to achieve immediate and lasting change in their lives.

Classroom challenge

TASK 15 - Digital Literacy

Instructions

1. Select one of the following organisations and visit their official website at the address shown below.
   Oxfam: www.oxfam.org.uk
   UNICEF: www.unincef.org.uk
   Save the Children: www.savethechildren.org.uk
   United Nations: www.un.org

2. You should find the following information from their website and record it in your jotter:
   - the organisation's aim and objectives
   - how the organisation raises awareness of their cause
   - how the organisation raises finance
   - the logo used by the organisation
   - an outline of any major issue/crisis where the organisation has given assistance
   - how effective their assistance has been
3. You should now present your findings in a PowerPoint presentation.
4. You should print your presentation in handout form ensuring your name is clearly displayed in a page footer.
5. You may have the opportunity to present your findings to a group.

TASK 16

Instructions

Select one of the countries shown below:

- Japan
- USA
- China
- Germany
- France

Go online to research your chosen country.
You should find out the following information:

- What goods/services does the country specialise in providing?
- Does the country have well-known companies with brands known worldwide?
- The main goods and services that these countries export.
- What countries do they trade with?

Present your findings in a PowerPoint presentation.

TEACHING NOTES

A template for Task 17 below can be downloaded from www.brightredpublishing.co.uk

TASK 17

The table below outlines some ways in which globalisation impacts on our lives. Complete the table below in your workbook by ticking (✔) the appropriate box to indicate whether the impact is positive or negative.

Impact	Positive	Negative
UK consumers enjoy a greater variety of goods and services.		
Pollution may increase.		
Greater road congestion caused by transporting goods from one country to another.		
Jobs are created for UK citizens.		
UK firms could go out of business if they cannot compete with foreign firms selling in the UK.		
UK citizens may be able to purchase cheap imported goods from abroad.		
Large multinational businesses may become too powerful and threaten local UK businesses.		

EMPLOYMENT AND TECHNOLOGY

The UK's **employment** structure has changed dramatically over the years. Historically, **primary sector** jobs, such as farming, were the most common. A key impact of the Industrial Revolution was that, by 1900, more than half of UK workers were employed in the **secondary** (or manufacturing) sector. Steelworks and ship building were common industries and many people found steady work.

By the year 2000, more than half of the UK workforce were employed in **tertiary** (or service) industries. Scotland is today a well-developed tourism destination with many jobs being provided in the service sector.

UNIT 6: EMPLOYMENT AND TECHNOLOGY

I can present conclusions about the impact of the globalisation of trade on patterns of work and conditions of employment in Scotland, the UK or beyond. SOC 3-20b

What's coming up?

Learning Intentions

In this unit of work, you will learn about:

- the primary sector
- the secondary sector
- the tertiary sector
- changes to UK working practices
- the impact of technology on individuals and businesses.

Success Criteria

To be successful with this unit of work you should:

- complete activities
- develop key skills in decision making, organisation and team working
- develop literacy, numeracy and digital literacy skills
- participate in class/group discussions
- provide your teacher with evidence of all the work that you have undertaken.

CHANGES IN EMPLOYMENT TRENDS

The UK's **employment** structure has changed dramatically over the years.

Early types of employment

Primary Sector

Centuries ago, **primary** sector jobs such as farming and other more traditional jobs were most common. However, these jobs began to phase out following the Industrial Revolution. More and more people began to move from the countryside to towns and cities in search of jobs.

The Industrial Revolution brought steam-powered engines, factories, machinery and trains. These helped make many changes for the better in the workplace. Many children were employed in Victorian factories because they were cheap and small enough to crawl under machines. It was dangerous work and they risked getting caught in the machinery and suffering serious injuries.

Young boys and girls working in a spinning room of a mill in 1912.

Classroom challenge

TASK 1 - Digital Literacy -Video Clip/ Discussion

Go online to the Bright Red website for a short video clip on The Industrial Revolution.

Discuss with a friend what opportunities you think were made available to Scotland following the Revolution.

Changes following the rise of technology and the Industrial Revolution

Secondary Sector

By 1900, more than half of UK workers were employed in the **secondary** (or manufacturing) sector. Steelworks and ship building were common industries and many people found steady work. Glasgow was famous for its Clydeside Shipyards along the banks of the Clyde and built many famous ships and other landmarks such as the Finnieston Crane over the years. However, following the Second World War and having suffered much devastation through intense bombing, the shipping industry went into decline.

The Finnieston Crane on the River Clyde, Glasgow.

DON'T FORGET

The UK had also suffered what was known as the 'Great Depression' in the 1930s, which saw a huge increase in unemployment and the secondary sector beginning to decline.

Present Times

Tertiary sector

By the year 2000, more than half of the UK workforce were employed in **tertiary** (or service) industries. Scotland is a well-developed tourism destination with many jobs being provided in the service sector.

People are attracted to visit Scotland for its rich history, scenery, golf, fishing, Highland games and food and drink. Many visitors come to Scotland to trace their ancestors and visit historical sites. More recently, Scotland has become known as a popular location for filming movies. This also attracts tourists who then visit the sites for themselves.

Classroom challenge

TASK 2 - Digital Literacy - Creative Thinking - PowerPoint - Solo Activity

Go to the Visit Scotland website – https://www.visitscotland.com/ - and research what Scotland has to offer visitors. Create a short PowerPoint which aims to promote Scotland to tourists from other countries.

Ensure you include images, animation and a suitable design layout. Save as Visit Scotland and print one copy of your PowerPoint.

TASK 3 - Digital Literacy - Creative Thinking - Poster - Solo Activity

Using the information that you researched on the Visit Scotland website, create a one-page poster using desktop publishing software of your choice to promote a popular tourist attraction in Scotland.

Ensure your poster makes use of different formatting styles, images, colours, a page border if you wish and any other enhancement to ensure your poster is eye-catching. Save as Attraction and print one copy of your poster.

Classroom challenge

TASK 4 - Problem Solving - Identifier - Solo Activity

Look at the list below and place each one within the correct sector of industry in the diagram below. You can complete this in your workbook.

ACCOUNTANCY	STEEL-MAKING	TEACHING	QUARRYING
CONSTRUCTION	CUSTOMER SERVICE	CABINET-MAKER	TRAVEL AGENT
FAST FOOD RESTAURANT	FISHING FORESTRY	DRESSMAKING	CAR PRODUCTION
LAWYER	MANUFACTURING	HAIRDRESSING	FARMING

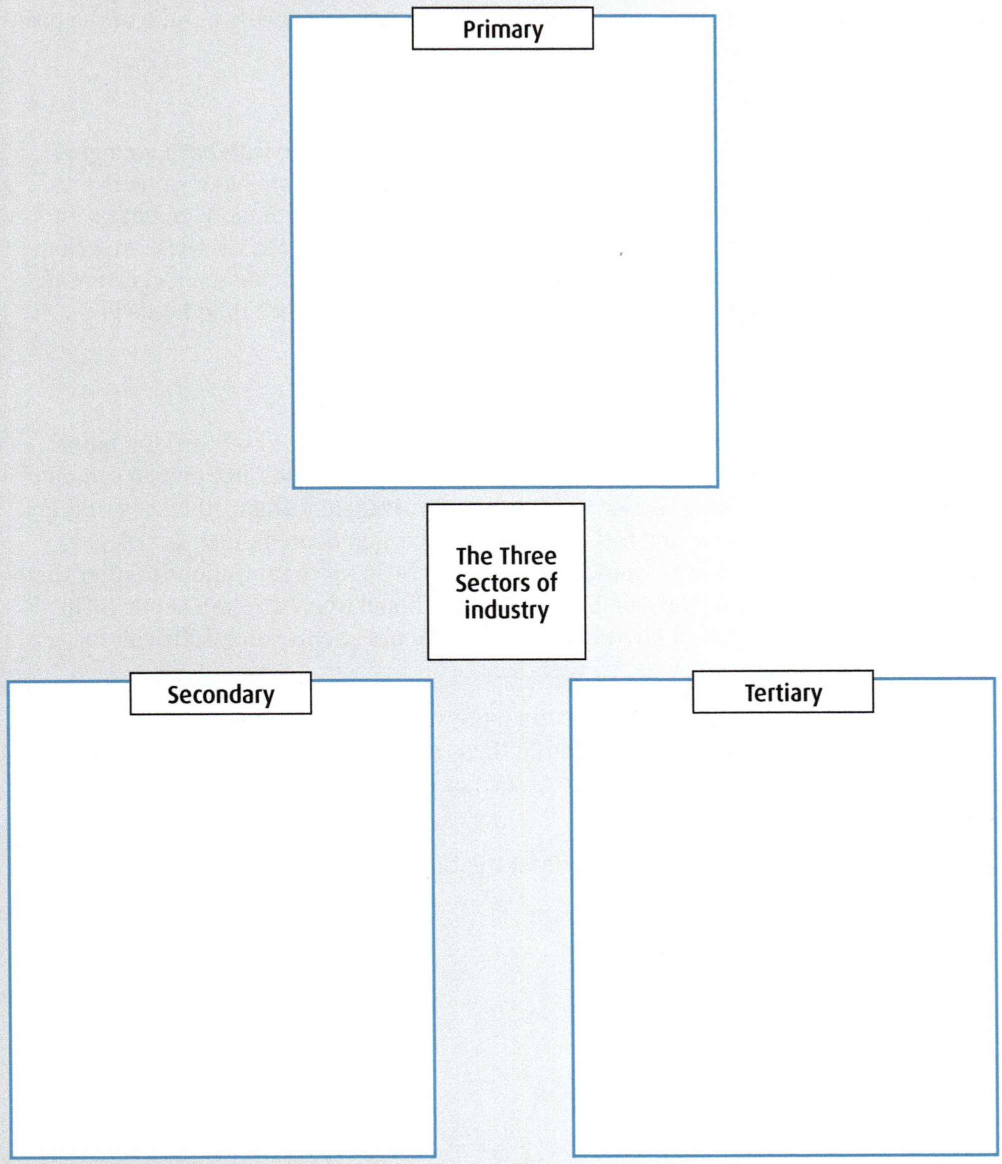

Let's look at Literacy - Keywords

Keyword	Definition
Primary sector	This sector of industry is concerned with making direct use of natural resources to create a product. Examples of primary sector industries include food, cars and clothes.
Secondary sector	Making a product using raw materials and using machinery and workers to create a finished product. Examples of secondary sector industries include food processing, oil refining and energy production.
Tertiary sector	The selling of services and skills as well as selling goods and services from primary and secondary sector industries. Examples of tertiary sector industries include transport, tourism and banking.

THE UK WORKPLACE

The workplace has seen many changes over the decades with the traditional 9 to 5 working day and roles of male managers with female assistants being a thing of the past. There have also been changes in patterns in working.

Part-time workers

Part-time workers make up a large percentage of the population with both younger and older generations taking advantage of these positions as more older workers are choosing to work reduced hours for longer periods. There is much more emphasis on equality, and more women now than ever before are making up the UK workforce. Some people might not be based in their place of work five days a week but instead can work from home; others can choose their own hours and so can balance their home life around their career.

Zero-hours workers

Zero-hours contract workers are workers who are not guaranteed set working hours but who instead get work when needed, so at certain 'busy periods' like during summer or Christmas, they will find it easier to get work. Unfortunately, this also means workers are not guaranteed any pay and this does not offer certain benefits such as sick pay. It's becoming more and more common because it's cheap for organisations to offer this type of flexible working as they simply pay workers if and when they are needed. The organisation is not obliged to provide any working hours so this can be difficult for workers to get enough money to pay their bills.

Both of these types of working practice are more suited to those looking for casual work such as students or working parents who fit these more flexible working hours around raising their children. Many organisations such as Cineworld and Sports Direct use zero-hours contracts.

The employee must be paid at the very least the National Minimum Wage regardless of how many hours are offered to them.

Classroom challenge

TASK 5 - Digital Literacy - Paired Activity

Go online and click on the following link to find out how much the current National Minimum Wage is.

https://www.gov.uk/national-minimum-wage-rates

Write this in your workbook. Are you surprised? Did you think it would be more or less? Discuss your thoughts with a partner.

Gig Economy

There is also a growing working practice known as the **'gig economy'**. This is when workers just get paid for the 'gigs' they do instead of receiving a monthly salary. Jobs that may be classed as being in the gig economy include couriers, food deliverers or Uber drivers.

Job-Hopping

Nowadays people 'job hop' every couple of years instead of committing their careers to one company alone. A lot of these changes are due to technological advances. The 'traditional office' no longer exists; the workplace of today is drastically different.

Classroom challenge

TASK 6 - Digital Literacy - Creative Thinking - Paired Discussion

Considering the changes that have occurred over the past decades, what do you imagine future workplaces could be like?

Write your thoughts in your workbook and discuss with a partner.

TECHNOLOGY AND BUSINESSES

Digital technology has helped shape many of these changes that businesses now take advantage of. This has enabled the world as we know it to become a 'smaller place'. It was 1990 when Tim Berners-Lee created the World Wide Web. A lot has changed since then!

Remember that as more and more of us have an increased online/social media presence, messages and photographs that we post can be seen by everyone, including future employers! Before you post anything, think twice as once it's on the internet, it's there for all to see.

Many people like to buy goods and services on the internet. This allows consumers to have more choice and benefit from cheaper prices. It also allows businesses to cut out expensive costs such as high street stores by building cheaper websites. Buying and selling online is known as **e-commerce**.

DON'T FORGET

Stay safe. As it is impossible to control what people post online, it is important to be aware that not everything you read or everyone you speak to is genuine!

Classroom challenge

TASK 7

Answer the following questions in your workbook.

1. State the year the World Wide Web was introduced.
2. Name three items the World Wide Web has enabled us to share with other Internet users.
3. Name two examples of social media platforms.
4. Explain why it is important that we think carefully about what we post online.
5. State what is meant by the term 'e-commerce'.

TASK 8 - Digital Literacy - Solo Activity

McDonald's is a global brand fast food outlet with restaurants in many countries all over the world.

Answer the following questions in your workbook.

1. Name three countries (not UK) where you might be able to visit a McDonald's restaurant.
2. Name a product sold by McDonald's overseas but which is not available in the UK. (You may wish to use the internet to help you with this task)

SCOTLAND'S GROWING INDUSTRY

Tourism is a big reason why people choose to visit Scotland. Whether it is for leisure pursuits such as playing golf or enjoying a dram of whisky or to take in the scenic side, tourism brings in over £4 billion to our economy every year.

A growing Tourism industry has created an increase in employment as more businesses are introduced to cater for the needs of foreign visitors.

Classroom challenge

Task 9 - Creative Thinking - Paired Discussion

Working with a partner, copy and complete the table below into your workbook.

Examples of jobs created by the Tourism industry.

The first two examples have been given for you.

1. air stewards	6.	11.
2. hotel staff	7.	12.
3.	8.	13.
4.	9.	14.
5.	10.	15.

Task 10 - Creative Thinking - Paired Discussion

Edinburgh and Glasgow are two major Scottish cities that tourists like to visit. Having large numbers of tourist in these cities can cause problems for local residents. Working with a partner, copy and complete the table below into your workbook.

Problems caused by tourists

Two examples have been given for you.

1. Overcrowded or fully booked restaurants
2. Pollution from increased flights and use of public transport
3.
4.
5.

SOFTWARE PACKAGES

The most common software packages you might use are word processing, presentations, spreadsheets and databases. These packages enable users to perform certain tasks when the package is installed on their device.

GENERAL-PURPOSE APPLICATION PACKAGES

A general-purpose application package is a type of software that can perform many different related tasks. Word processors, spreadsheets, databases and presentation software are all examples of application packages.

Word Processing Software

This is text processing software used to create various business documents such as letters, reports, displays and posters. Once text has been entered, formatting functions such as size, colour, bold, italics, underline, different sizes, page borders and different colours can be used to enhance the appearance of the document.

Spreadsheet Software

A spreadsheet package is a general-purpose package (GPP) used to carry out **calculations** and to investigate what happens if **data** changes. Microsoft® Excel is an example of a spreadsheet package.

Spreadsheets are made up of **cells**. A cell is where a column and row meet. Each cell has an **address** made up of the **column letter** and the **row number**. This is known as the **cell reference**. For example, in the spreadsheet shown below **cell B6** is in **column B** and **row 6**.

DON'T FORGET

Spreadsheets can hold **data** such as text or numbers or **formulae**.

	A	B	C	D	E	F
1	**TOTAL MONTHLY INCOME FOR MARCH**					
2		**Week 1**	**Week 2**	**Week 3**	**Week 4**	**Total**
3	Pet Sales	£150.00	£220.00	£250.00	£190.00	£810.00
4	Food Sales	£75.00	£90.00	£120.00	£140.00	£425.00
5	Accommodation	£230.00	£300.00	£370.00	£330.00	£1,230.00
6	**Total**	£455.00	£610.00	£740.00	£660.00	£2,465.00

Database Software

A database is a collection of information relating to a particular subject or purpose, for example, details of a music collection including artists and names of tracks and albums or pupils' personal details held on a school's database.

Databases contain **tables of information.**

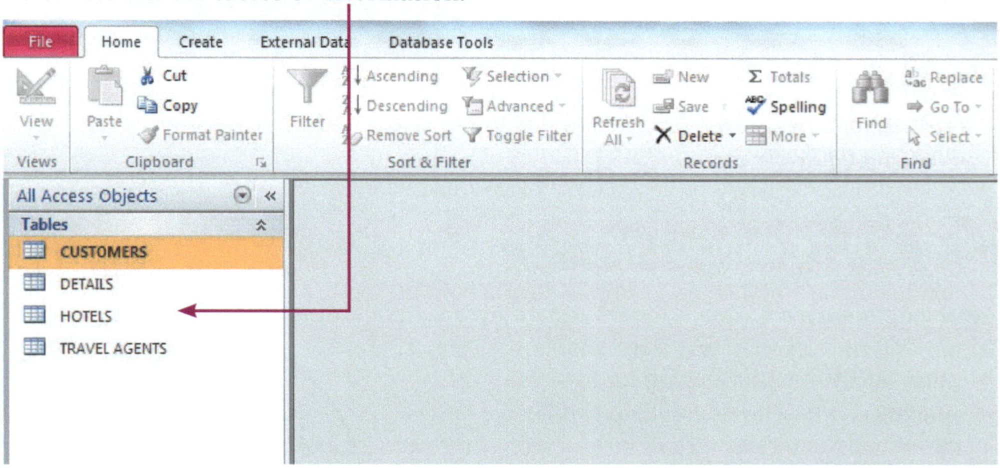

These **tables** are made up of **records** and each record is divided into **fields.**

FIELDS

RECORDS

First Name	Surname	Street	Town	Postcode	Date of Birth	Tutor Group	Emergency Contact Name
Jane	Black	23 South Scott Street	Baillieston	G69 8UH	18/11/95	3L4	Mr Sam Black
Joan	Brown	39 Kirk Street	Mount Vernon	G69 7HU	31/07/95	3M3	Mrs Joan Brown
Guy	Ford	28 Main Street	Baillieston	G69 4HY	23/10/95	3T2	Mrs Wendy Ford
Peter	Green	16 Camp Road	Baillieston	G69 5OP	20/09/95	3B2	Ms Jess Green
John	Smith	45 Rosedale Drive	Baillieston	G69 8HY	15/01/96	3M3	Mrs Jean Smith

This is an example of a **table of information. Fields** can be formatted, for example, for text or number or date or currency (£), etc. **Fields** can be **sorted,** for example, into alphabetical order of surname.

Presentation Software

PowerPoint presentations are used to present information on a screen, usually at a meeting. A PowerPoint presentation consists of a number of slides, containing information, graphs or charts and pictures. Animations such as sound can be added to a PowerPoint presentation. The presenter presents his or her presentation to an audience using a computer, digital projector and a large screen.

WORD PROCESSING

I can explore the impact, contribution and use of various software applications and emerging hardware in business. SOC 3-08

What's coming up?

Learning Intentions
In this unit of work, you will learn about:
- using bullets and numbering for lists
- creating, formatting and editing simple business documents
- inserting graphics
- inserting headers and footers.

Success Criteria
Creating a range of documents which demonstrate that you can:
- use watermarks/graphics
- use different formats and font styles
- insert page borders
- create a document following a house style
- insert headers and footers
- provide your teacher with evidence of all the work that you have undertaken.

BULLETS AND NUMBERING

Try some of these tasks which will test your knowledge of bullets and numbering as well as your skills in changing fonts, line spacing, text formatting and layout.

Instructions for Tasks 1-6

1. Set left and right margins to 2.5 cm.
2. Use the line spacing indicated.
3. Key in the text and follow all editing instructions.
4. When you have completed the task, use the **spellcheck** and proofread for any errors.
5. Save each task using the file name provided and print.

Classroom challenge

TASK 1

Countries of the World   caps and bold

- France
- Spain
- Portugal
- USA

Use bullet points as shown

Save as Countries.

TASK 2

TRAINING PROGRAMME – ADMINISTRATIVE SERVICES DEPARTMENT   bold

Course   u/score

Your course will include –

1. Word Processing
2. Spreadsheets
3. Databases
4. Electronic Mail
5. Internet

number the display section at the left margin

All members of staff should inform their line manager what area of the course is their main priority.

Save as Technology.

TASK 3

Use a font of your choice for this exercise

Open Day   caps

Come along and join in! Attractions include:

- Guided walks
- Falconry Exhibitions
- Pageants
- Craft Stalls

Bullet this list at the left margin

Save as Activities.

TASK 4

HEALTH AND SAFETY Bold

Workers are protected by:

The Health and Safety at Work Act 1974 Use a larger font size

Employers have a duty to provide a safe workplace for employees.

The following steps should be taken to prevent accidents:

- Keep the fire exits clear.
- Do not leave fire doors ajar.
- Keep floors and stairways in good repair.
- Close filing cabinets when not in use.
- Switch off electrical appliances.

Use bullet points of your choice and double line spacing for the display section.

Please ensure that any breach of the above rules is reported to the Safety Officer.

Save as Safety.

TASK 5

Customer Service Bold and caps

Good customer service means:

1. Happy customers who will keep coming back to the organisation
2. Happy staff who will stay with the organisation and do a good job
3. A good reputation for the organisation which will attract new customers
4. Increased sales and higher profits

Number these items at the margin and u double line spacing this section

Save as Customer.

TASK 6

SKILLS AND QUALITIES OF AN ADMINISTRATIVE ASSISTANT Bold

ʎ able A skill is something you are ʎ to do. The skills of an Administrative Assistant include:

- ICT skills
- communication skills
- problem solving skills
- teamwork skills

Use two different types of bullets

A quality describes what kind of person you are. The qualities of an Administrative Assistant include:

- organised
- keen to learn
- polite
- helpful and friendly

Save as Skills.

NOTICES AND DISPLAYS

Classroom challenge

TASK 7

1. Create the notice shown below
2. All text should be centred horizontally
3. Add a graphic or watermark
4. Make use of different formats and add a page border
5. Insert your name in the footer and save the document as ***DISPLAY 7***
6. Print one copy of the document

Ponderosa Pets Bold
Stronach Farm
Denholm Road
Hawick
>2LS
For all your pet accessories:
>2LS
Food
Straw
Hay
Sawdust
Cages
Toys
>3LS
Holiday your pet with us – it'll have fun when you're in the sun! Underline
>3LS
Pets for sale:
>2LS
Mice
Guinea pigs
Hamsters
Gerbils
Rabbits
Rats
>2LS
Telephone: 01450 552234

Below is a basic example of a notice for reference

Rosebank Riding School
Rosebank Farm
Moodiesburn

OPEN DAY

SATURDAY 29 JUNE 20xx
From 10 am until 5 pm

Come along and join the fun!

Tombola
Bouncy Castle
Face Painting
Cake and Candy Stall
Barbeque
Pony Rides
Equipment and Accessories Stalls
Book 6 lesson for the price of 5!

Raffle with grand prize of free riding lessons!

TASK 8

1. Create the notice shown below
2. All text should be <u>centred horizontally</u>
3. Add a graphic or a watermark
4. Make use of different formats and add a page border
5. Insert your name in the footer and save the document as ***DISPLAY 8***
6. Print one copy of the document

Bathgate Bairns Caps
>3LS
Presents
>3LS
2022 Easter Bunny Hunt
>2LS
in
>2LS
Halfacre Country Park
>2LS
Starting at 2.30pm
>2LS
On
>2LS
Sunday 14 April 20--
>2LS
Lots of prizes for the children including Underline
>2LS
Toys
Sweets
Easter Eggs
Easter Bunny for each participant

TASK 9

1. Create the notice shown below
2. All text should be centred horizontally
3. Add a graphic or a watermark
4. Make use of different formats and add a page border
5. Insert your name in the footer and save the document as ***DISPLAY 9***
6. Print one copy of the document

You are invited to an
Entertainment Extravaganza Bold
hosted by
Jonathan Wilson
Art of Entertainment
Come along to
Ardleigh House Hotel
Great Western Road
Aberdeen
On Friday 17 May 20-- Italics and Bold
at 7.30pm Italics and Bold
During the evening you will be entertained by many of our fabulous acts including:
Burnbank Ceilidh Band
Razzamataz
Peter and the Pistachios
Party Time
Come early to avoid disappointment and dance away the evening to some of our hottest sounds!

TASK 10

1. Create the notice shown below
2. All text should be centred horizontally
3. Add a graphic or a watermark
4. Make use of different formats and add a page border
5. Insert your name in the footer and save the document as ***DISPLAY 10***
6. Print one copy of the document

MUNRO MOTORS Bold
27 HIGH STREET
KINROSS
Family Barbeque Day Italics and underline
Saturday 27 July 20--
Fun starts at 11.00am
Burgers and Hot Dogs
Raffles
Bouncy Castle
Lucky Dips
Mystery Guest Caps

Classroom challenge

TASK 11

1. Open the letterhead **NORTHGATE COMMUNITY CENTRE**
2. Key in the business letter shown below
3. Put your name in the header and save the letter as ***Task 18***
4. Print one copy of the letter

RC/own initials
>2LS
Today's date
>2LS
Mrs Sylvia Main
14 Limetree Lane
DUNDEE
DD7 4ER
>2LS
Dear Sylvia
>2LS
JEWELLERY MAKING
>2LS
I am pleased to say that 22 people have shown an interest in joining your jewellery making group at the Centre.

The Committee is, at the moment, finalising the timetable of classes. Please contact me to confirm that Tuesday evenings are still suitable for you.

The programme will start the week commencing Monday 13 May. If you have any questions before then please do not hesitate to get in touch.
>2LS
Yours sincerely
>6LS
Richard Cameron
Chairperson
Insert the following text in the centre of the footer – use bold and italics:
The beating heart of Northgate!

BUSINESS LETTERS

Below is an example of a business letter for reference

BUSINESS LETTER LAYOUT

>3LS (whenever you see LS, it means you press the return key. You would press it three times here)

JD/Your initials (This is the letter reference with two sets of initials. The first set is who the letter is from and the second set are yours)

>2LS

Today's date **(**eg: 21 February 20--**)**

>2LS

Mr J L Jones
35 Wilton Lane
NEWTOWN
N45 8NB

>2LS

Dear Mr Jones

>2LS

OFFICE EQUIPMENT

>2LS

Thank you for your enquiry about our new range of office equipment. We are pleased to enclose our brochure, and note below some of our special offers.

>3LS

2-drawer filing cabinet	£49.90
Pedestal desk	£89.99
Typist chair	£34.50

>3LS

All of the above prices exclude VAT, and represent a saving of 25% on our normal prices.

If you require any more information, please telephone us on the above number. We look forward to receiving your first order.

Yours sincerely (if there is no name to address the letter to you would type Yours faithfully)

>6LS

Jane Dawson
Sales Director

>3LS

Enc

Keyed in if letter refers to any enclosures if anything is included in the envelope

TASK 12

1. Open the letterhead **BELLA PIZZERIA**
2. Key in the business letter shown below
3. Put your name in the footer and save the letter as ***Task 19***
4. Print one copy of the letter

MV/own initials
>2LS
Today's date
>2LS
Mrs J Harvey
Booking Manager
Catering Training Services Ltd
986 Dunkeld Drive
PERTH
PH1 5BD
>2LS
Dear Mrs Harvey
>2LS
LEVEL 1 FOOD HYGIENE TRAINING COURSE
>2LS
Thank you for the food hygiene training course information. I have read the information supplied and am satisfied that the Level 1 Food Hygiene Course meets all of our basic training requirements.

I would like to book a place for our trainee chef, Miss Summer Jones, on the Level 1 course scheduled to take place in your Perth offices on Wednesday 1 May 20--.

Please find enclosed a cheque for £250 in full payment of course fees.

Yours sincerely
>6LS
Madison Volpe
Manager
>3LS
Enc

TASK 13

1. Open the letterhead **FIRST STEPS NURSERY**
2. Key in the business letter shown below
3. Put your name in the header and save the letter as ***Task 20***
4. Print one copy of the letter

MK/own initials
>2LS
Today's date
>2LS
Ms Sandra Taylor
14 Lilac Grove
ST ANDREWS
KY16 7TU
>2LS
Dear Ms Taylor
>2LS
SAFETY AT THE NURSERY
>2LS
Thank you for your recent comments regarding entry and exit to and from the Nursery.

We have decided to bring the important points you have made to the attention of all parents/guardians who are dropping off and collecting children. We will be reminding all people entering and leaving our premises to ensure that the door is firmly closed behind them. We will also be highlighting the importance of discouraging children from touching the security button beside the door. Parents/guardians will be asked to inform any extended family, who are picking up their children, of the importance of these issues.

Thank you again for bringing this to our attention.
>2LS
Yours sincerely
>6LS
Morven Knox
Senior Play Leader
Insert the following text in the centre of the footer – use bold and caps:
LEARNING THROUGH PLAY

TASK 14

1. Open the letterhead **GREENACRE HOLIDAY PARK**
2. Key in the business letter shown below
3. Put your name in the header and save the letter as ***Task 22***
4. Print one copy of the letter

MG/own initials
>2LS
Today's date
>2LS
Mrs K Myres
365a Hunter Street
KIRKCALDY
KY1 3HJ
>2LS
Dear Mrs Myres
>2LS
ACCOMMODATION ENQUIRY–PARTY OF 30
>2LS
Thank you for your recent enquiry. I am pleased to inform you that we have a selection of caravans available for booking which match your required dates (Monday 5 August – Friday 9 August 20--).

We have 4 standards of caravan for hire: platinum, gold, silver and bronze. The bronze standard caravans are our budget range and are very popular with youth groups and other parties. All of our caravans cater for 6 persons; therefore, you would need to book 5 caravans for your group of 30.

I have enclosed details of our prices, which also show some of our special rates.

Please do not hesitate to contact me if I can be of further help.

We hope to see you in August 20--.
>2LS
Yours sincerely
>6LS
Martin Green
Owner
>3LS
Enc
Insert the following text at the left side of the footer – use comic sans and bold:
Rest and relaxation in a woodland setting

SPREADSHEETS

I can explore the impact, contribution and use of various software applications and emerging hardware in business. SOC 3-08

What's coming up?

Learning Intentions

In this unit of work, you will learn about:

- editing a worksheet
- using formulae including subtraction, multiplication, division and Autosum
- formatting cells
- inserting and deleting a row
- unhiding a column
- printing a worksheet showing values and formulae with/without gridlines and row and column headings
- creating a chart using data from a spreadsheet
- labelling and printing a chart.

Success Criteria

Creating a range of documents which demonstrate that you can:

- use appropriate formulae to make simple calculations
- delete and insert rows to a workbook
- produce a variety of labelled charts
- display data showing value and formulae views.

WORKING WITH SPREADSHEETS

Try some of these tasks which will test your skills at editing data, working with rows and columns and creating charts.

EDITING DATA

TEACHING NOTES

Files for Tasks 1-4 can be downloaded from the Bright Red website www.brightredpublishing.co.uk

Classroom challenge

TASK 1 - Editing data

Open the spreadsheet **USAGE**. Change the data as follows:

- Change 'Games Hall' in cell **A4** to 'Gym'
- The number of people using Room 4 on a Tuesday should be 10 not 0. Change the figure in cell **C8**. *You should notice that the total in cell C9 will now be 102 not 92 and the total in cell G9 will now be 470 not 460.*
- Save the file as *Task 1*
- Print one copy of the worksheet showing the corrected figures.

DON'T FORGET

Ensure you include gridlines only for Task 1 to Task 6.

TASK 2 - Editing data

Open the spreadsheet **EXPENSES**. Change the data as follows:

- Change the heading 'SECOND QUARTER EXPENSES' to 'THIRD QUARTER EXPENSES'
- Training expenses in September should be £149.00 – change the figure in cell **D5**. *Note that as these cells have been formatted to currency you **DO NOT** key in the £ sign.*
- *Check that the total in cell E5 is now £494.00 and the overall total in cell E10 is £13,500.00*
- Save the file as *Task 2*
- Print one copy of the worksheet showing the corrected figures.

TASK 3 - Editing data

Open the spreadsheet **DOLOMITES**. Change the data as follows:

- Change the main heading in cell **A1** to read 'GORLOWSKI TOURS'
- The deposit in cell **C12** should be 10% not 5% – change this figure. *Note that as this cell has been formatted to percentage you **DO NOT** key in the % sign.*
- *Check that the amount in cell D12 is now £200.00 and the overall total amount to pay in cell D13 is £1,800.00*
- Save the file as *Task 3*
- Print one copy of the worksheet showing the corrected figures.

TASK 4 - Editing data

Open the spreadsheet **SUNDRIES**. Change the data as follows:

- Change the month in cell **A2** to read 'JULY'
- The cost of flowers in cell **C9** should be £9.50 not £7.50 – change this figure. *Note that as these cells have been formatted to currency you* ***DO NOT*** *key in the £ sign.*
- *Check that the amount in cell D9 is now £38.00, the overall total in cell D11 is £182.55 and the result of the percentage calculation in cell D13 is now 9.59%*
- Save the file as *Task 4*
- Print one copy of the worksheet showing the corrected figures.

TASK 5 - Editing data

Open the spreadsheet **SALARY**. Change the data as follows:

- Change the job title in cell **A6** to read 'Admin Assistant'
- The salary of Warehouse Staff in cell **C8** should be £12,000 not £10,000 – change this figure. *Note that as these cells have been formatted to currency you* ***DO NOT*** *key in the £ sign.*
- *Check that the amount in cell D8 is now £60,000 and the Overall Salary Cost in cell D9 is now £391,000*
- Save the file as *Task 5*
- Print one copy of the worksheet showing the corrected figures.

TASK 6 - Editing data

Open the spreadsheet **MEMBERSHIP**. Change the data as follows:

- Change the type of member in cell **A5** to read 'Junior'
- The membership fee for a Junior cell **C5** should be £5 not £3 – change this figure. *Note that as these cells have been formatted to currency you* ***DO NOT*** *key in the £ sign.*
- *Check that the amount in cell D5 is now £170, the overall total in cell D8 is £1,700 and the results of the percentage calculation in cell D9 is now 10%*
- Save the file as *Task 6*
- Print one copy of the worksheet showing the corrected figures – ensure you include gridlines only.

WORKING WITH ROWS

Classroom challenge

TASK 7 - Inserting a row and using AutoSum (Σ)

Open the spreadsheet file **DAILY ATTENDANCES** and carry out the instructions below.

- Insert a blank row between row 1 and row 2 – your worksheet will now look like the one below

	A	B	C	D
1	DAILY ATTENDANCES			
2				
3		Afternoon	Night	TOTAL
4	Screen 1	235	422	?
5	Screen 2	167	312	?
6	Screen 3	315	524	?
7	TOTAL	*=SUM(B4:B6)*	?	?

- Use the AutoSum button (Σ) on the toolbar to calculate totals in those cells marked with a question mark (?)
- *Study the worksheet above – you will see an example of the formula you should be using*
- Put your name in the footer – File menu, Page Setup, Header/Footer, Custom Footer
- Save the spreadsheet as *Task 7*
- Print one copy of Task 7 showing formulae – ensure your printout shows gridlines and row and column headings.

TASK 8 - Inserting a row and using AutoSum (Σ)

Open the spreadsheet file **BANNERMAN NURSERY** and carry out the instructions below.

- Insert a blank row between rows 1 and 2 – your worksheet will now look like the one below

	A	B	C	D	E	F	G
1	NO. OF CHILDREN ATTENDING IN JANUARY						
2							
3		**Mon**	**Tue**	**Wed**	**Thu**	**Fri**	**Total**
4	Week 1	8	9	5	10	11	**?**
5	Week 2	8	9	5	8	11	**?**
6	Week 3	9	11	12	10	7	**?**
7	Week 4	7	9	10	12	4	**?**
8	**Total**	**?**	**?**	**?**	**?**	**?**	**?**

- Use the AutoSum button (Σ) on the toolbar to calculate totals in those cells marked with a question mark (?)
- Put your name in the footer – File menu, Page Setup, Header/Footer, Custom Footer
- Save the spreadsheet as *Task 8*
- Print one copy of Task 8 showing formulae – ensure your printout shows gridlines and row and column headings.

TASK 9 - Inserting a row and using AutoSum (Σ)

Open the spreadsheet **INVERNESS ROYALS** and carry out the instructions below.

- Insert a row between row 2 and 3 – your worksheet will now look like the one below

	A	B	C	D	E
1	INVERNESS ROYALS				
2	**GOALS SCORED THIS SEASON**				
3					
4		**League**	**Cup**	**Friendly**	**Total**
5	Macdonald	3	4	2	**?**
6	Stevens	0	1	0	**?**
7	Martin	4	3	0	**?**
8	Walters	0	0	2	**?**
9	Greaves	0	0	2	**?**
10	Total	**?**	**?**	**?**	**?**

- Use the AutoSum button (Σ) on the toolbar to calculate totals in those cells marked with a question mark (?)
- Put your name in the footer – File menu, Page Setup, Header/Footer, Custom Footer
- Save the spreadsheet as *Task 9*
- Print one copy of Task 9 showing formulae – ensure your printout shows gridlines and row and column headings.

TASK 10 - Inserting a row and using AutoSum (Σ)

Open the spreadsheet **MITSUKI CARS** and carry out the instructions below.

- Insert a blank row between rows 1 and 2
- Use the AutoSum button (Σ) on the toolbar to calculate totals in those cells marked with a question mark (?)

	A	B	C	D	E
1	**ESTIMATED MONTHLY SALES OF NEW CARS**				
2					
3		**January**	**February**	**March**	**Total**
4	1200 cc	8	7	7	**?**
5	1600 cc	6	4	5	**?**
6	1800 cc	3	5	5	**?**
7	2400 cc	0	2	4	**?**
8	Estate	0	2	3	**?**
9	**Total**	**?**	**?**	**?**	**?**

- Put your name in the footer – File menu, Page Setup, Header/Footer, Custom Footer
- Save the spreadsheet as *Task 10*
- Print one copy of Task 10 showing formulae – ensure your printout shows gridlines and row and column headings.

TASK 11 - Inserting a row, using AutoSum (Σ) and formatting for currency

Open the spreadsheet **PONDEROSA PETS** and carry out the instructions below.

- Insert a blank row between rows 1 and 2
- **Ensure cells are formatted as currency to two decimal places (cells B4:F7)** – your worksheet will look like the one below

	A	B	C	D	E	F
1	**TOTAL MONTHLY INCOME FOR MARCH**					
2						
3		**Week 1**	**Week 2**	**Week 3**	**Week 4**	**TOTAL**
4	Pet Sales	£150.00	£220.00	£250.00	£190.00	?
5	Food Sales	£75.00	£90.00	£120.00	£140.00	?
6	Accommodation	£230.00	£300.00	£370.00	£330.00	?
7	**Total**	?	?	?	?	?

- Use the AutoSum button (Σ) on the toolbar to calculate totals in those cells marked with a question mark (?)
- Put your name in the footer – File menu, Page Setup, Header/Footer, Custom Footer
- Save the spreadsheet as *Task 11*
- Print one copy of Task 11 showing figures – ensure your printout shows gridlines

TASK 12 - Deleting a row, using AutoSum (Σ) and subtraction (-)

Open the spreadsheet **WALLPAPER** and carry out the instructions below.

- Delete row 3 – your worksheet will look like the one below

	A	B	C	D
1	WALLPAPER SALES			
2				
3	Design	August Sales	July Sales	Difference in Sales
4	Flora	£32,000	£24,750	*=B4-C4*
5	Spiral	£19,510	£15,750	?
6	Vintage	£10,980	£5,460	?
7	Riva	£6,500	£4,570	?
8	TOTAL	*=SUM(B4:B7)*	?	?

- Key in a formula to calculate the difference in sales between August and July in those cells marked with a question mark (?)
- Hint: your formula should be **=B4-C4**
- Use the AutoSum button (Σ) on the toolbar to calculate totals in those cells marked with a question mark (?)

Study the worksheet above – you will see examples of the formulae you should be using.

- Put your name in the footer – File menu, Page Setup, Header/Footer, Custom Footer
- Save the spreadsheet as *Task 12*
- Print one copy of Task 12 showing formulae – ensure your printout shows gridlines and row and column headings.

TASK 13 - Deleting a row, using AutoSum (Σ) and subtraction (-)

Open the spreadsheet **SAVINGS** and carry out the instructions below.

- Delete row 4 – your worksheet will look like the one below

	A	B	C	D
1	SAVINGS ACCOUNT			
2	*Brian's Savings Account*			
3		2018	2017	Difference Between Years
4	January	£60	£40	?
5	February	£100	£75	?
6	March	£80	£60	?
7	April	£75	£40	?
8	May	£66	£43	?
9	June	£75	£55	?
10	TOTAL	?	?	?

- Key in a formula to calculate the difference in Brian's savings between 2018 and 2017 in those cells marked with a question mark (?)
- Hint: your formula should be **=B4-C4**
- Use the AutoSum button (Σ) on the toolbar to calculate totals in those cells marked with a question mark (?)
- Put your name in the footer – File menu, Page Setup, Header/Footer, Custom Footer
- Save the spreadsheet as *Task 13*
- Print one copy of Task 13 showing formulae – ensure your printout shows gridlines and row and column headings.

TASK 14 - Deleting a row, using AutoSum (Σ) and subtraction (-)

Open the spreadsheet **STATIONERY** and carry out the instructions below.

- Delete row 3 – your worksheet will look like the one below

	A	B	C	D
1	BANNERMAN STATIONERS' SALES COMPARISON			
2				
3		2018	2017	Difference in Sales
4	A4 lined paper packs	£56,001	£37,569	?
5	Gel Pens	£47,523	£36,789	?
6	Photo Print Packs	£14,531	£12,312	?
7	TOTAL	?	?	?

- Key in a formula to calculate the difference in sales between 2018 and 2017 in those cells marked with a question mark (?)
- Hint: your formula should be = **B4-C4**
- Use the AutoSum button (Σ) on the toolbar to calculate totals in the cell marked with a question mark (?)
- Put your name in the footer – File menu, Page Setup, Header/Footer, Custom Footer
- Save the spreadsheet as *Task 14*
- Print one copy of Task 14 showing formulae – ensure your printout shows gridlines and row and column headings.

TASK 15 - Deleting a row, using AutoSum (Σ) and subtraction (-)

Open the spreadsheet **RESULTS** and carry out the instructions below.

- Delete row 5 – your worksheet will look like the one below

	A	B	C	D
1	EXAM RESULTS COMPARED			
2	Number of Pupil Passes			
3	Subject	2018	2017	Difference Between Years
4	English	350	273	?
5	Maths	375	363	?
6	History	85	56	?
7	PE	125	89	?
8	TOTAL	?	?	?

- Key in a formula to calculate the difference in the number of pupil passes between 2018 and 2017 in those cells marked with a question mark (?)
- Hint – your formula should be = **B5-C5**
- Use the AutoSum button (Σ) on the toolbar to calculate totals in the cell marked with a question mark (?). ***Be careful not to include the column headings 2018 and 2017 in your calculations!***
- Put your name in the footer – File menu, Page Setup, Header/Footer, Custom Footer
- Save the spreadsheet as *Task 15*
- Print one copy of Task 15 showing formulae – ensure your printout shows gridlines and row and column headings.

TASK 16 - Deleting a row and subtraction (-)

Open the spreadsheet **SUNSHINE** and carry out the instructions below.

- Delete row 5 – your worksheet will look like the one below

	A	B	C	D
1	SUNSHINE HOLIDAYS			
2	*Sale*			
3				
4	Place	Price Before Discount	Discount	New Price
5	Majorca	£456.99	£151.99	?
6	Paris	£445.00	£120.00	?
7	Marbella	£645.99	£245.99	?

- Key in a formula to calculate the new price of the holidays in those cells marked with a question mark (?)
- Hint – your formula should be **=B5-C5**
- Put your name in the footer – File menu, Page Setup, Header/Footer, Custom Footer
- Save the spreadsheet as *Task 16*
- Print one copy of Task 16 showing figures – ensure your printout shows gridlines
- Print one copy of Task 16 showing formulae – ensure your printout shows gridlines and row and column headings.

WORKING WITH COLUMNS

Classroom challenge

TASK 17 – Unhiding a column, using AutoSum (Σ) and multiplication (*)

Open the spreadsheet **GYM** and carry out the instructions below.

- Unhide column D – your worksheet will look like the one below

	A	B	C	D
1	GYM FIGURES FOR WEEK BEG 2 FEBRUARY			
2		Daily Attendance	Entrance Fee	Daily Income
3	Monday	223	£1.25	*=B3*C3*
4	Tuesday	344	£1.25	?
5	Wednesday	*421*	£1.25	?
6	TOTAL	*=SUM(B3:B5)*		?

- Key in a formula to calculate the daily income in those cells marked with a question mark (**?**)
- Hint – your formula should be **=B3*C3**
- Use the AutoSum button (S) on the toolbar to calculate totals in the cells marked with a question mark (**?**)
- Ensure cells are formatted appropriately
- Study the worksheet above – you will see examples of the formulae you should be using
- Put your name in the footer – File menu, Page Setup, Header/Footer, Custom Footer
- Save the spreadsheet as *Task 17*
- Print one copy of Task 17 showing formulae – ensure your printout shows gridlines and row and column headings.

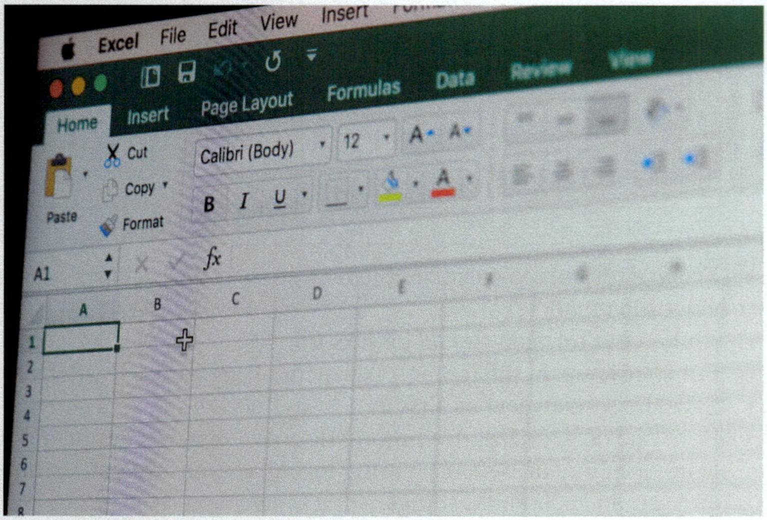

TASK 18 - Unhiding a column, using AutoSum (Σ) and multiplication (*)

Open the spreadsheet **PETS** and carry out the instructions below.

- Unhide column D – your worksheet will look like the one below

	A	B	C	D
1	PET SHOP – SALES WEEK 1			
2		Quantity Sold	Price per Animal	Weekly Income
3	Hamster	24	£6.00	?
4	Goldfish	44	£3.50	?
5	Guinea Pig	10	£11.00	?
6	TOTAL	?		?

- Key in a formula to calculate the weekly income in those cells marked with a question mark (?)
- Hint – your formula should be **=B3*C3**
- Use the AutoSum button (Σ) on the toolbar to calculate totals in those cells marked with a question mark (?)
- Ensure cells are formatted appropriately
- Put your name in the footer – File menu, Page Setup, Header/Footer, Custom Footer
- Save the spreadsheet as *Task 18*
- Print one copy of Task 18 showing formulae – ensure your printout shows gridlines and row and column headings.

TASK 19 - Unhiding a column, using AutoSum (Σ) and multiplication (*)

Open the spreadsheet **SCHOOL SHOW** and carry out the instructions below.

- Unhide column D – your worksheet will look like the one below

	A	B	C	D
1	SCHOOL SHOW			
2				
3	Day	Tickets Sold	Ticket Price	Ticket Income
4	Tuesday	250	£3.50	?
5	Wednesday	225	£3.50	?
6	Thursday	275	£4.00	?
7	TOTAL	?		?

- Key in a formula to calculate the ticket income in those cells marked with a question mark (?)
- Hint – your formula should be **=B4*C4**
- Use the AutoSum button (Σ) on the toolbar to calculate totals in the cells marked with a question mark (?)
- Ensure cells are formatted appropriately
- Put your name in the footer – File menu, Page Setup, Header/Footer, Custom Footer
- Save the spreadsheet as *Task 19*
- Print one copy of Task 19 showing formulae – ensure your printout shows gridlines and row and column headings.

TASK 20 - Unhiding a column, using AutoSum (Σ) and multiplication (*)

Open the spreadsheet **BEAUTY SALON** and carry out the instructions below.

- Unhide column D – your worksheet will look like the one below

	A	B	C	D
1	BEAUTY SALON			
2				
3	Name	Normal Weekly Hours	Rate of Hourly Pay	Salary
4	Jamil	40	£7.99	?
5	Max	38	£5.99	?
6	Lucy	40	£3.99	?
7	TOTAL	?		?

- Key in a formula to calculate the salary in those cells marked with a question mark (**?**)
- Hint – your formula should be **=B4*C4**
- Use the AutoSum button (**Σ**) on the toolbar to calculate totals in the cells marked with a question mark (**?**)
- Ensure cells are formatted appropriately
- Put your name in the footer – File menu, Page Setup, Header/Footer, Custom Footer
- Save the spreadsheet as *Task 20*
- Print one copy of Task 20 showing formulae – ensure your printout shows gridlines and row and column headings.

TASK 21 - Unhiding a column, using AutoSum (Σ) and multiplication (*)

Open the spreadsheet **CARS** and carry out the instructions below.

- Unhide column E – your worksheet will look like the one below

	A	B	C	D	E
1	CAR SHOWROOM – JUNE SALES				
2					
3	Manufacturer	Model	Quantity	Price per Car	Income
4	Vauxhall	Corsa	5	£9,999	?
5	Nissan	Micra	3	£7,999	?
6	Peugeot	306	2	£12,999	?
7	Honda	Civic	4	£14,999	?
8	TOTAL		?		?

- Key in a formula to calculate the income in those cells marked with a question mark (**?**)
- Hint – your formula should be **=C4*D4**
- Use the AutoSum button (Σ) on the toolbar to calculate totals in those cells marked with a question mark (**?**)
- Ensure cells are formatted appropriately
- Put your name in the footer – File menu, Page Setup, Header/Footer, Custom Footer
- Save the spreadsheet as *Task 21*
- Print one copy of Task 21 showing formulae – ensure your printout shows gridlines and row and column headings.

TASK 22 - Unhiding a column, using AutoSum (Σ) and multiplication (*)

Open the spreadsheet **MAGAZINE** and carry out the instructions below.

- Unhide column D – your worksheet will look like the one below

	A	B	C	D
1	HI MAGAZINE – QUARTERLY SALES			
2				
3	Monthly Edition	Number of Magazines Sold	Price per Magazine	Sales Income
4	January	17,256	£3.99	?
5	February	24,589	£3.99	?
6	March	20,048	£3.99	?
7	April	17,004	£4.99	?
8	TOTAL	?		?

- Key in a formula to calculate the sales income in those cells marked with a question mark (**?**)
- Hint – your formula should be **=B4*C4**
- Use the AutoSum button (Σ) on the toolbar to calculate totals in those cells marked with a question mark (**?**)
- Ensure cells are formatted appropriately
- Put your name in the footer – File menu, Page Setup, Header/Footer, Custom Footer
- Save the spreadsheet as *Task 22*
- Print one copy of Task 22 showing formulae – ensure your printout shows gridlines and row and column headings.

DELETING ROWS

Classroom challenge

TASK 23 - Deleting a row, using AutoSum (Σ) and division (/)

Open the spreadsheet **FASHION** and carry out the instructions below.

- Delete row 3 – your worksheet will look like the one below

	A	B	C	D
1	NEW FASHION – WEEK 1 SALES			
2				
3	Item	Sales Income	Price	Quantity Sold
4	Denim skirts	£114.95	£22.99	*=B4/C4*
5	Cardigans	£111.93	£15.99	?
6	Boots	£119.97	£39.99	?
7	TOTAL	=SUM(B4:B6)		?

- Key in a formula to calculate the quantity sold in those cells marked with a question mark (?)
- Hint – your formula should be **=B4/C4**
- Use the AutoSum button (Σ) on the toolbar to calculate totals in those cells marked with a question mark (?)
- Ensure cells are formatted appropriately
- Study the worksheet above – you will see examples of the formulae you should be using
- Put your name in the footer – File menu, Page Setup, Header/Footer, Custom Footer
- Save the spreadsheet as *Task 23*
- Print one copy of Task 23 showing formulae – ensure your printout shows gridlines and row and column headings.

TASK 24 - Deleting a row, using AutoSum (Σ) and division (/)

Open the spreadsheet **VETS** and carry out the instructions below.

- Delete row 3 – your worksheet will look like the one below

	A	B	C	D
1	VET CENTRE – MONTHLY WAGES			
2				
3	Vet Name	Monthly Wage	Rate Paid per Animal Treated	Number of Animals Treated
4	Elisa	£1,500.00	£50.00	?
5	Billy	£1,800.00	£75.00	?
6	Sameena	£1,200.00	£30.00	?
7	TOTAL	?		?

- Key in a formula to calculate the number of animals treated in those cells marked with a question mark (**?**)
- Hint – your formula should be **=B4/C4**
- Use the AutoSum button (Σ) on the toolbar to calculate totals in the cells marked with a question mark (**?**)
- Ensure cells are formatted appropriately
- Put your name in the footer – File menu, Page Setup, Header/Footer, Custom Footer
- Save the spreadsheet as *Task 24*
- Print one copy of Task 24 showing formulae – ensure your printout shows gridlines and row and column headings.

TASK 25 - Deleting a row, using AutoSum (Σ) and division (/)

Open the spreadsheet **BAKERY** and carry out the instructions below.

- Delete row 3 – your worksheet will look like the one below

	A	B	C	D
1	BAKERY – WEEK 1 SALES			
2				
3	Item	Sales Income	Price per Item	Quantity Sold
4	Yum Yum	£25.00	£1.25	?
5	Éclair	£30.00	£1.20	?
6	Meringue	£40.00	£2.00	?
7	TOTAL	?		?

- Key in a formula to calculate the quantity sold in those cells marked with a question mark (?)
- Hint – your formula should be **=B4/C4**
- Use the AutoSum button (Σ) on the toolbar to calculate totals in those cells marked with a question mark (?)
- Ensure cells are formatted appropriately
- Put your name in the footer – File menu, Page Setup, Header/Footer, Custom Footer
- Save the spreadsheet as *Task 25*
- Print one copy of Task 25 showing formulae – ensure your printout shows gridlines and row and column headings.

CHARTING

Classroom challenge

TASK 26 - Charting: column chart

You wish to create a column chart to show the hours worked by staff at Bannerman Nursery during the month of February.

- Open a new worksheet and enter the data below

	A	B
1	**HOURS WORKED DURING FEBRUARY**	
2	**Staff Member**	**Number of Hours**
3	Stewart	52
4	Frank	18
5	Jasmine	34
6	Paul	65
7	Jack	15
8	Fiona	18

- Create a column chart using the chart wizard
- Move the chart to a separate sheet
- The chart should have the following title: **HOURS WORKED DURING FEBRUARY**
- Label the horizontal axis: **Staff Member**
- Label the vertical axis: **Number of Hours**
- Put your name in the footer – File menu, Page Setup, Header/Footer, Custom Footer
- Save the spreadsheet as *Task 26*
- Print one copy of your chart.

TASK 27 - Charting: pie chart

Rosebank Riding School would like you to create a pie chart showing the income they received from classes and stabling during January.

- Open a new worksheet
- Enter the data below

	A	B
1	**INCOME FOR OCTOBER**	
2	**CLASS**	**INCOME**
3	Group Lessons	£1,680
4	Private Lessons	£4,075
5	Jump Academy	£1,600
6	Stabling	£8,000
7	Dressage	£800

- Create a pie chart on a separate sheet
- The title of the pie chart should be: **INCOME FOR OCTOBER**
- Label your pie chart with percentages
- ***Hint*** – go to ***Chart Tools***, ***Layout***, ***Data Labels*** then ***More Data Labels Options*** and select ***Percentage***
- Ensure your legend indicates the lessons/stabling/jump academy
- Put your name in the footer – File menu, Page Setup, Header/Footer, Custom Footer
- Save the spreadsheet as *Task 27*
- Print one copy of your pie chart.

TASK 28 - Charting: column chart

La Plaza cinema wants you to produce a chart showing the average daily income received during the afternoon and during the evening.

- Open a new worksheet and enter the data below

	A	B	C
1	**AVERAGE DAILY INCOME**		
2		**Afternoon**	**Evening**
3	Mon	£230	£460
4	Tue	£270	£400
5	Wed	£456	£585
6	Thu	£345	£565
7	Fri	£380	£900
8	Sat	£890	£1,200
9	Sun	£650	£800

- Create a column chart using the chart wizard

***Hint**: you will need to highlight all the column headings as well as all the data*

- The chart should have the following title: **AVERAGE DAILY INCOME**
- Label the horizontal axis: **Day**
- Label the vertical axis: **Income**
- **Ensure the legend is displayed**
- Put your name in the footer
- Save the spreadsheet as a separate sheet as *Task 28*
- Print one copy of your chart.

TASK 29 - Charting: pie chart

Mr and Mrs Robertson are taking a trip to the Dolomites and would like a breakdown of their costs displayed as a pie chart.

- Open a new worksheet and enter the data below

	A	B
1	**COST STATEMENT FOR MR AND MRS ROBERTSON**	
2	**ITEM**	**TOTAL COST**
3	Flights	£545.00
4	Transfers	£46.50
5	Hotel (BB)	£145.50
6	Trek Accommodation	£263.00
7	Travel Insurance	£60.00

- Create a pie chart
- The title of the pie chart should be: **TRIP COSTS – MR AND MRS ROBERTSON**
- Label your pie chart with the percentage values for each item
- Put your name in the footer – File menu, Page Setup, Header/Footer, Custom Footer
- Save the spreadsheet *Task 29*
- Print one copy of your pie chart.

TASK 30 - Charting: bar chart

Create a bar chart to show the total spending on sundry items by Lorelle's Luxury Limos for the month of August – these are items that are included in the limos that are hired for a variety of events.

- Open a new worksheet and enter the data below

	A	B
1	**SUNDRIES EXPENDITURE – AUGUST**	
2	**Item**	**Total Amount**
3	Fruit Juices	£75.60
4	Soft Drinks	£17.50
5	Chocolates	£21.75
6	Children's Sweets	£20.00
7	Fresh Flowers	£34.00
8	Ribbon	£8.25

- Create a bar chart using the chart wizard
- Move the chart to a separate sheet
- The chart should have the following title: **SUNDRIES EXPENDITURE – AUGUST**
- Label the horizontal axis: **Total Amount**
- Label the vertical axis: **Item**
- Put your name in the footer – File menu, Page Setup, Header/Footer, Custom Footer
- Save the spreadsheet as *Task 30*
- Print one copy of your chart.

TASK 31 - Charting: column chart

Richard Muldrow, Store Manager of the furniture retailer LifeStyle, wants you to create a column chart showing total salary costs for the business.

- Open a new worksheet and enter the data below

	A	B
1	**ANNUAL STORE SALARY COST**	
2	**POSITION**	**SALARY**
3	Manager	£48,500
4	Depute Manager	£62,000
5	Senior Admin Assistant	£18,500
6	Admin Assistant	£42,000
7	Showroom Staff	£160,000
8	Warehouse Staff	£60,000

- Create a column chart using the chart wizard
- The chart should have the following title: **ANNUAL STORE SALARY COST**
- Label the horizontal axis: **Position**
- Label the vertical axis: **Salary**
- Put your name in the footer
- Save the spreadsheet as a separate sheet as *Task 31*
- Print one copy of your chart.

DATABASES

I can explore the impact, contribution and use of various software applications and emerging hardware in business. SOC 3-08

What's coming up?

Learning Intentions

In this unit of work, you will learn about:

- amending/deleting/inserting a field
- changing field format – text, number, currency, date/time, yes/no
- amending/deleting/inserting a record
- sorting a database table on one field
- printing on one page.

Success Criteria

Creating a range of documents which demonstrate that you can:

- recall database tables and set different field types
- amend records
- sort a database
- print tables
- provide your teacher with evidence of all the work that you have done.

WORKING WITH DATABASES

Try some of these tasks which will test your skills adding and deleting records, changing values and changing formats.

ADDING AND DELETING RECORDS

Classroom challenge

Task 1A

- Recall the database *La Plaza Cinema* and open the table of information called *Golden Bratpack Club Members*
- Change the **format** of the Member field to **number**
- Add a new field called Senior Member – **this should be formatted as a Yes/No field** – and add the following information:

Second Name	First Name	Senior Member
Smith	Darren	No
Jones	Chloe	Yes
Ali	Hussain	No
Stewart	Jordan	No
Wilson	Jason	Yes
Rashid	Jenny	No
Miller	Leeann	No
Dawson	Koni	Yes
Ahmed	Nita	No
Brown	Wayne	Yes

- Change the field name Area to Town
- Sort the database into alphabetic order of second name
- Print one copy of the table by exporting to Word. Ensure you use **AutoFit to Window** so that you can see all the text. Put your name in the footer before you print.

Task 1B

Now make the following changes to the *Golden Bratpack Club Members* table:

- Jordan Stewart has left the area – delete his record
- A new Senior Member has been admitted to the club – add a new record to hold his details:
  Karl Forbes
  22 Fife Way
  Torry
  Karl's telephone number is 473916
  He will be given the next membership number – 11
- Leeann Miller has moved house – her new address is 26 Keith Street, Kincorth. Her telephone number remains the same
- Sort the database into alphabetic order of town and print one copy of the table on one page.

TEACHING NOTES

The files for the following tasks can be downloaded from the Bright Red website www.brightredpublishing.co.uk

Task 2A

- Recall the database *Munro Motors* and open the table of information called Cars
- Change the **format** of the Engine (cc) field to **number**
- Change the **format** of the Price (£) field to **currency**
- Add a new field called MOT Due – **this should be formatted as a Date field** – and add the following information:

Make	Model	MOT Due
Toyota	Supra	31/01/2019
Peugeot	406	15/02/2019
Peugeot	306	15/01/2019
Ford	Focus	26/09/2019
Honda	Accord	17/06/2019
Ford	Mondeo	25/04/2020
Rover	Metro	04/02/2020
Nissan	Primera	25/07/2019
VW	Golf	03/08/2020
Ford	Focus	06/08/2019
Renault	Scenic	29/07/2019
Ford	Mondeo	03/10/2019

- Sort the database into alphabetic order of make
- Print one copy of the table by exporting to Word. Ensure you use **AutoFit to Window** so that you can see all the text. Put your name in the footer before you print.

Task 2B

Now make the following changes to the Cars table:

- The following cars have been sold – delete the records:
  Peugeot 406
  Rover Metro
  Nissan Primera
- Reduce the price of the VW Golf from £8500 to £8000
- A car has been taken in part exchange – enter the details into the database:

Make	Vauxhall
Model	Vectra
Engine (cc)	2500
Type	Saloon
Price (£)	£7950
Reg No	X21 TDU
MOT Due	26.08.2020

- Sort the database into alphabetic order of model and print one copy of the table on one page.

Task 3A

- Recall the database *Inverness Royals Football Club* and open the table of information called Staff
- Change the **format** of the Salary field to **currency**
- Change the **format** of the Employee Ref to **number**
- Add a new field called Date of Start – **this should be formatted as a date field** – and add the following information:

Surname	First Name	Date of Start
Davidson	Gordon	04/04/2015
Cumming	John	17/06/2017
Adams	David	27/06/2010
Thomson	Andrew	20/10/2013
Thomson	Abigail	18/11/2017
Forsyth	Maureen	23/09/2017
Black	Rona	05/02/2016
Campbell	Margaret	16/07/2018
Zerouali	Rashid	14/05/2018
Khan	Ashraf	13/12/2017
Wallace	Lee	14/03/2018
Macdonald	Donnie	26/07/2017

- Sort the database into alphabetic order of responsibility
- Print one copy of the table by exporting to Word. Ensure you use **AutoFit to Window** so that you can see all the text. Put your name in the footer before you print.

Task 3B

Now make the following changes to the Staff table:

- Abigail Thomson has recently married – change her surname to Struthers
- Rona Black and Maureen Forsyth have left to start their own business. Delete their records
- A new employee has joined the club – details are as follows:

Surname	Finlayson
First Name	Mary
Employee Ref	236
Telephone Number	511237
Responsibility	Marketing
Salary (£)	20,000
Date of Start	Today's date

- Lee Wallace has completed his course at college. Increase his salary to £12,000
- Sort the database into alphabetic order of surname and print one copy of the table on one page.

Task 4A

- Recall the database *Ponderosa Pets* and open the table of information called Employees
- Change the **format** of the Staff No field to **number**
- Change the **format** of the Wage Rate field to **currency**
- Add a new field called Permanent – **this should be formatted as a Yes/No field** – and add the following information:

First Name	Surname	Permanent
Jim	Grant	Yes
Anne	Forsyth	Yes
Wilma	Ferguson	No
Janet	Morgan	No
Maggie	Devlin	Yes
Jack	Cook	Yes
Stewart	Main	No
Javed	Rahman	No
Ian	Harris	Yes
Ali	Patel	Yes
Bill	Thomson	Yes
Mandy	Smith	Yes

- Change the field name Hours to Status
- Sort the database into ascending order of wage rate
- Print one copy of the table by exporting to Word. Ensure you use **AutoFit to Window** so that you can see all the text. Put your name in the footer before you print.

Task 4B

Now make the following changes to the Employees table:

- Jack Cook has moved to Edinburgh and will no longer be working for us. Delete his record
- Janet Morgan has moved house. Her new phone number is 500121
- Denise Jones has started working for us on a temporary basis. Her staff number is 199, her telephone number is 556212 and she will be part time, earning £5 per hour
- Sort the database into alphabetical order of surname and print one copy of the table on one page.

Task 5A

- Recall the database *Bathgate Bairns* and open the table of information called Children
- Change the **format** of the Age field to **number**
- Change the **format** of the Lunch Club field to **Yes/No**
- Add a new field called Emergency Contact – **this should be formatted as a text field** – and add the following information:

First Name	Surname	Emergency Contact
Suzanne	Brown	Louise
Jack	Wareham	Fiona
Chloe	Daniels	Jack
Imran	Khan	Jatinder
Rebekah	McKay	Iona
Julie	Mathieson	Angela
Alastair	Connors	James
Patrick	McNee	Jennifer
Alison	Lewis	Peter
Darren	Fletcher	Keith
Kylie	McNaughton	Sheila
Bobby	Robertson	John

- Sort the database into alphabetic order of surname
- Print one copy of the table by exporting to Word. Ensure you use **AutoFit to Window** so that you can see all the text. Put your name in the footer before you print.

Task 5B

Now make the following changes to the Children table:

- Darren Fletcher and his family have moved to Inverness. Delete his record
- Chloe Daniels is now aged 4. Update her record
- Peter Fox has joined the nursery. He is aged 3 and the contact name is Frank. He will be attending the lunch club and his phone number is 334481
- Sort the database by age, oldest first and print one copy of the table on one page.

Task 6A

- Recall the database *Highland Amusements* and open the table of information called Arcade Machines
- Change the **format** of the No. of Machines field to **number**
- Add a new field called Maintenance Due – **this should be formatted as a Yes/No field** – and add the following information:

Machine Name	Maintenance Due
Wild Rapids	Yes
Road Rage	No
Waterfall	Yes
Soccer 2003	No
Golf World	No
Bandit Country	No
Evil Cats	Yes
Rally Wild	No
Grand Prix	Yes
Frogger	Yes
Grand Canyon	No
Flying High	Yes

- Sort the database into alphabetic order of manufacturer
- Print one copy of the table by exporting to Word. Ensure you use **AutoFit to Window** so that you can see all the text. Put your name in the footer before you print.

Task 6B

Now make the following changes to the Arcade Machines table:

- The Grand Canyon machines have been sold – delete this record
- Another Waterfall machine has been bought. Update this record
- A new game machine called Storm Rae, manufactured by Wega, has been bought from Anderson & Co. The contact there is Jimmy
- Suzie has left Games plc and has been replaced by Kylie
- **Hint**: you can use the **Find and Replace** feature

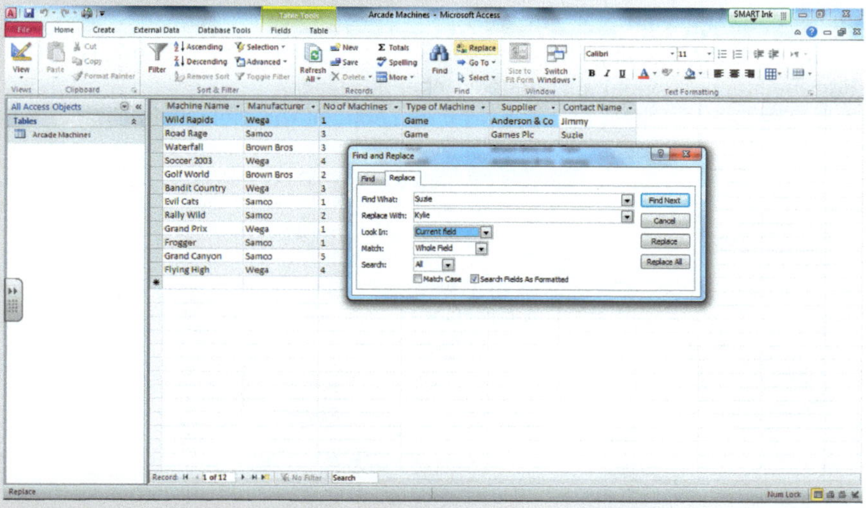

- Sort the database by no. of machines, highest first. Print one copy of the table on one page.

Task 7A

- Recall the database *Kincardine Cleaning Services* and open the table of information called Employee Information
- Change the **format** of the Staff No. field to **number**
- Change the **format** of the First Aid Certificate field to **Yes/No**
- Add a new field called Tel No. – **this should be formatted as a Text field** – and add the following information:

Surname	First Name	Tel No
Chapman	Beth	07788 8645391
Lanois	Danny	07898 8639002
Purcell	Katie	08789 8860803
Black	Mary	07788 8645334
Silver	Michael	07973 8823935
Alexander	Lee	07788 8753126
Mwelase	Jabulani	08789 8657447
Pallot	Nerin	08789 8652218
Shaw	Donald	07788 8664729
Sayal	Indira	07973 8865672

- Sort the database into ascending order of Staff No.
- Print one copy of the table by exporting to Word. Ensure you use **AutoFit to Window** so that you can see all the text. Put your name in the footer before you print.

Task 7B

Now make the following changes to the Employee Information table:

- Mary Black has left the area. Delete her record
- Katie Purcell has been promoted to Grade A
- A new employee has been hired. Details are given below:

Surname	Thile
First Name	Chris
Staff No	301
First Aid Certificate	Yes
Grade	B
Tel No	07788 8661751

- Nerin Pallot has gained her First Aid Certificate
- Sort the database into descending order of surname. Print one copy of the table on one page.

Task 8A

- Recall the database *Borders Employment Agency* and open the table of information called Temporary Job Vacancies
- Change the **format** of the Rate field to **currency** with two decimal places
- Change the **format** of the No. of Days to **number**
- Some jobs may become permanent – add a new field called Permanent Vacancy – **this should be formatted as a Yes/No** field – and add the following information:

Reference	Permanent Vacancy
REC12	Yes
SEC24	No
WPO26	Yes
OFJ20	No
CLE33	No
DOG3	No
REC15	Yes
CLE39	Yes
TEC10	No
REC16	Yes

- Sort the database into alphabetic order of location
- Print one copy of the table by exporting to Word. Ensure you use **AutoFit to Window** so that you can see all the text. Put your name in the footer before you print.

Task 8B

Now make the following changes to the Temporary Job Vacancies table:

- The Dog Groomer vacancy has been filled – delete this record
- The WP Operator vacancy (Reference WPO26) has been changed to ten days and the rate has been increased to £7
- A new vacancy has to be added to the database. Details are as follows:

Job Title	Administrative Assistant
Location	Peebles
Reference	ADM17
Rate (£)	8
Employer	John Walker Travel
Contact Name	Drew
No of Days	10
Permanent	Yes

- Cindy has left Oracle Ltd and has been replaced by Anna
- Sort the database in alphabetical order of job title. Print one copy of the table on one page.

Task 9A

- Recall the database *Carnoustie Cats Volleyball Club* and open the table of information called Club Players
- Change the **format** of the Shirt No. field to **number**
- Change the **format** of the Subs Paid to **Yes/No**
- Add a new field called Subs Due – **this should be formatted as currency** and inserted after the field Team. Add the following information:

First Name	Surname	Subs Due
Rocco	Deluca	£25.00
Ramon	Estevez	£25.00
Julius	Marx	£25.00
Phil	Liggett	£25.00
Teddy	Thompson	£25.00
Joan	Osbourne	£22.50
Rosie	Thomas	£22.50
Jacqui	Dankworth	£22.50
Jamie	Hunter	£25.00
Frankie	Miller	£25.00
Marie	Lawrie	£22.50
Sarah	Harmer	£22.50

- Sort the database into alphabetic order of team
- Print one copy of the table by exporting to Word. Ensure you use **AutoFit to Window** so that you can see all the text. Put your name in the footer before you print.

Task 9B

Now make the following changes to the Club Players table:

- Jamie Hunter has left the area – delete this record
- In the Team field, Women is to be changed to Ladies
- **Hint**: you can use the **Find and Replace** feature (see Task 6B on page 140)
- A new player has to be added to the database. Details are as follows:

First Name	Michael
Surname	Cortese
Shirt No	5
Telephone No	956888
Team	Men
Subs Due	£25.00
Subs Paid	Yes

- Sarah has recently married; her surname is now Euringer
- Sort the database in alphabetical order of surname. Print one copy of the table on one page.

Task 10A

- Recall the database *Bella Pizzeria* and open the table of information called Employee Details
- Change the **format** of the Hours field to **number**
- Change the **format** of the Trained? to **Yes/No**
- Add a new field called Date Started – **this should be formatted as date.** Add the following information:

First Name	Surname	Date Started
Ravinder	Kaur	12/06/2017
Stephen	Cairns	14/11/2016
Summer	Jones	04/09/2015
Madison	Volpe	16/12/2017
Matthew	Smith	06/06/2017
Ava	Glen	05/01/2018
Ethan	Taylor	13/08/2016
Zachary	Knight	15/09/2016
Lei	Sun	22/04/2017
Karolina	Jablonski	23/05/2018

- Sort the database into alphabetic order of job title
- Print one copy of the table by exporting to Word. Ensure you use **AutoFit to Window** so that you can see all the text. Put your name in the footer before you print.

Task 10B

Now make the following changes to the Employee Details table:

- Ava Glen has recently married. Change her surname to Locke
- Zachary Knight has been promoted to the position of Head Waiter. Change his details to show his new job title. His contracted hours are now 35 and his pay scale is B3
- A new employee has to be added to the database. Details are as follows:

First Name	Caitlin
Surname	Henderson
Employee Ref	M244
Job Title	Waitress
Hours	17
Pay Scale	A1
Trained?	No
Date of Start	12/05/16

- Stephen Cairns no longer works for the restaurant. Delete his record
- Sort the database in alphabetical order of surname. Print one copy of the table on one page.

Task 11A

- Recall the database *Green Acre Holiday Park* and open the table of information called Entertainers
- Change the **format** of the Equity Member field to **Yes/No**
- Add a new field called Rate per Hour – **this should be formatted as currency**. Add the following information:

Act Name	Rate per Hour
Mysterious	£12.50
The Terrible Tweenies	£15.00
Beat the Drum	£10.50
Dance to the Beat	£10.50
Hot Air	£11.00
Mr Fun	£10.50
Hand in Glove	£10.50
Space Pirate	£11.25
Mr Tumble	£10.50
The Doodlebugs	£12.00
Dance Station	£15.00
Watch my Lips	£10.50

- Sort the database by rate per hour – lowest to highest
- Print one copy of the table by exporting to Word. Ensure you use **AutoFit to Window** so that you can see all the text. Put your name in the footer before you print.

Task 11B

Now make the following changes to the Entertainers table:

- Hand in Glove have informed us that they are no longer in business. Please delete their record
- The Doodlebugs are now Equity members and their booking rate should be changed to £14.00
- A new act has to be added to the database. Details are as follows:

Booking Ref	13
Act Name	Seaside Entertainments
Act Type	Puppeteer
Contact Name	Harry
Contact Tel No	622975
Booking Rate	£10.50
Equity Member	No

- Alison is no longer the contact for The Terrible Tweenies – please amend the contact details. The new contact is Steven and his telephone number is 634417
- Sort the database in alphabetical order of act name. Print one copy of the table on one page.

Task 12A

- Recall the database *Rosebank Riding School* and open the table of information called Riders
- Change the **format** of the Grade field to **number**
- Add a new field called Passed – **this should be formatted as Yes/No**. Add the following information:

First Name	Surname	Passed
Courtney	Sullivan	Yes
Shannon	Walker	No
Rachel	Gorman	Yes
Julliette	Johnson	No
Piotr	Kempinska	Yes
Charlie	Price	Yes
Nicole	Robertson	Yes
Claire	Healy	Yes
Anna	Senior	No
Sean	Kennedy	Yes
Carla	Mazzucco	No
Eilish	Lowe	No

- Sort the database by town – descending
- Print one copy of the table by exporting to Word. Ensure you use **AutoFit to Window** so that you can see all the text. Put your name in the footer before you print.

Task 12B

Now make the following changes to the Riders table:

- Rachel Gorman has been moved up to Grade 2 and Claire Healy to Grade 3 – they have both still to pass this grade. Change their records accordingly
- A new rider has to be added to the database. Details are given below:

First Name	Jamie
Surname	Harrison
Address	8 Fifth Avenue
Town	Stepps
Postcode	G33 4WR
Grade	1
Passed	No

- Charlie Price has left the riding school. Delete his record
- Sort the database in alphabetical order of surname. Print one copy of the table on one page.

PRESENTATIONS

I can explore the impact, contribution and use of various software applications and emerging hardware in business. SOC 3-08

What's coming up?

Learning Intentions

In this unit of work, you will learn about:

- using slide layouts
- inserting text boxes
- using background styles and colour and design themes
- inserting graphics and images
- adding animations – special effects to keep your audience interested
- adding sound/video
- adding slide transitions – different ways to change from one slide to the next, for example, the current slide dissolves into the next one
- printing slides.

Success Criteria

To be successful with this unit of work you should:

- be able to complete a full presentation and present it to your class
- provide your teacher with evidence of all the work that you have undertaken.

PRESENTATIONS

Try some of these tasks which will test your skills at creating and developing presentations.

CREATING SLIDESHOWS

Classroom challenge

TASK 1 - Cities of the USA

Use presentation software to create a slideshow about cities of the USA.

<u>Slide 1 – Title Slide Layout</u>

- Select an appropriate Background Style and colour
- Using Word Art, insert and centre the heading: CITIES OF THE USA. Animate this heading
- Under the heading insert the subtitle: Mini Facts
- Insert a graphic of a map of the USA in an appropriate place
- Animate the main heading and the graphic.

<u>Slide 2 – Title and Content Layout with a bulleted list</u>

- Change the colour of the background for this slide and for the remaining slides
- Insert and centre the heading: WASHINGTON DC. Use a different font and put it in italics.
- Insert the following as a bulleted list:
  Population 7.6 million
  Area 9,567 square miles
  Average income $23,100
  Climate 37 degrees F (winter)
  Climate 77 degrees F (summer)

<u>Slide 3 – Title and Content Layout with a bulleted list</u>

- Insert the title: NEW YORK
- Insert the following as a bulleted list:
  Population 8 million
  Area 7,795 square miles
  Average Income $23,100
- Go online and search for an appropriate graphic to insert into the slide.
- Insert a text box and centre the following text below the bulleted list: One of the most densely populated cities in the USA
- Animate all text and the graphic.

Slide 4 – Title and Content Layout with a bulleted list

- Insert the title: SAN FRANCISCO
- Create the following bulleted list:
  Population 7 million
  Distance from London 3,572 miles
  Area 7,368 square miles
- Insert a picture sourced online of the Golden Gate Bridge
- Animate all text and the graphic.

Slide 5 – Title and Content Layout with a bulleted list

- Insert the title: LOS ANGELES
- Create the following bulleted list:
  Population 3.8 million
  Area 4,061 square miles
  Average income $20,683
- Search online for an appropriate graphic to insert into the slide
- Animate all text and the graphic

Slide 6 – Title and Content Layout with a table

- Insert the heading: OTHER PLACES TO VISIT IN THE USA
- Embolden and increase the size of the main heading
- Below the heading create the following table. Use a different font from the heading for the text in the table

Boston	Las Vegas	Florida
Philadelphia	Chicago	New Orleans
California	Houston	Minneapolis

All Slides

- Apply a slide transition to all slides

Email

- Email a copy of your presentation to your teacher.

TASK 2 - Gondwana Garden Centre

Use presentation software to create a slideshow for the Gondwana Garden Centre.

Slide 1 – Title Slide layout

- Select an appropriate Design Theme
- Using Word Art, insert and centre the heading: GARDENING. Apply suitable animation
- Under the heading insert the text: A Healthy Pursuit
- Insert a graphic in an appropriate place
- Animate the main heading and the graphic

Slide 2 – Two Content Layout with two columns

- Insert and centre the heading: HEALTH BENEFITS OF GARDENING
- Below the heading insert the following text in two columns

Heart disease	Obesity
Adult-onset diabetes	High blood pressure
Osteoporosis	

- Insert a text box and centre the following text below these columns: Regular exercise can prevent the onset of all of the above

Slide 3 – Title Only Layout

- Insert and centre the heading: AND IT'S GOOD TO EAT TOO!
- Insert the following passage on to the slide:
  Gardening provides the regular physical exercise listed in the prevention of heart disease, obesity, adult-onset diabetes and high blood pressure. It also provides the strength training important in the prevention of osteoporosis. Put a gallon sprinkling can full of water in each hand and you got your 8-pound dumbbells. Finish off with lifting a wheelbarrow and you got your bicep workout.

Slide 4 – Title and Content Layout with a table

- Insert and centre the heading: GETTING STARTED
- Below the heading create the following table. Embolden column headings and use a different font from the text in the rest of the table. Adjust the size of text as necessary

Seeds	**Recommended Retail Price**	**Special Offer**
Vegetable Seeds	£7.56	£2.99
Beetroot Detroit	£2.99	£1.79
Carrot Nantes	£2.50	£1.79
Coriander Seeds	£2.50	£1.79
Parsley Seeds	£2.50	£1.79

All Slides

- Apply a slide transition to all slides

Email

- Email a copy of your presentation to your teacher.

TASK 3 - Royal Academy of Music and Drama

Use presentation software to create a slideshow for the Royal Academy of Music and Drama.

Slide 1 – Title Slide Layout

- Select an appropriate Background Style and colour
- Insert and centre the heading: THE ORCHESTRA. Use a large font size and suitable animation
- Under the heading insert the subtitle: Guide to the Sections
- Insert a picture sourced online of an orchestra in an appropriate place
- Animate the main heading and the graphic

Slide 2 – Title Only Layout

- Insert and centre the heading: THE CONDUCTOR. Use a different font and format as italics
- Use a text box to enter the following information: Leads the orchestra, keeps time and shapes the music

Slide 3 – Two Content Layout with two columns

- Change the colour of the background for this slide and for the remaining slides
- Insert the title: STRINGS
- Create the following as a bulleted list in two columns: violin, viola, cello, double bass, harp
- Search online for an appropriate graphic to insert into the slide
- Animate all the text and the graphic
- Insert a text box and centre the following text below these columns: These instruments are essential to any orchestra

Slide 4 – Title and Content Layout

- Insert the title: WOODWIND
- Create the following bullet list: flute, clarinet, saxophone, oboe, bassoon
- Search online for an appropriate graphic to insert into the slide
- Animate all the text and the graphic

Slide 5 – Title and Content Layout with a bulleted list

- Insert the title: BRASS
- Create the following bullet list: trumpet, French horn, trombone, tuba
- Search online for an appropriate graphic to insert into the slide
- Animate all the text and the graphic

Slide 6 – Title and Content Layout with a table

- Insert the heading PERCUSSION INSTRUMENTS
- Below the heading create the following table. Use a different text font from the heading for the text in the table

xylophone	bass/side drums
glockenspiel	triangle
bells	timpani

All Slides

- Apply a slide transition to all slides

Email

- Email a copy of your presentation to your teacher.

TASK 4 - International Education

Use presentation software to create a slideshow for International Education.

Slide 1 – Title Slide Layout

- Select an appropriate Design Theme
- Insert and centre the heading: INTERNATIONAL CENTRE FOR INNOVATION IN EDUCATION. Increase the font size and apply animation
- Under the heading insert the text: Committed to the development of all learners as productive world citizens
- Search online for an appropriate graphic to insert into the slide
- Animate the main heading and the graphic

Slide 2 – Two Content Layout with two columns

- Insert and centre the heading: CONFERENCE AIMS AND OBJECTIVES
- Below the heading insert the following text in two columns

Encourage volunteer spirit	Promote excellence
Connecting communities	Strive for improvement
Evolve responsibility	Meet community expectations of quality
Sustain competitiveness and viability	Balance innovation with core essentials

- Insert a text box and centre the following text below this table: Global communities united in a common purpose

Slide 3 – Title Only Layout

- Insert and centre the heading: PRE-CONFERENCE WORKSHOPS
- Insert the following passage on to the slide:
  Pre-Conference workshops will be organized in two sessions. The first session starts at 9.00am and includes six workshops. The second session starts at 2.00pm and includes six workshops. It is recommended that you register for one workshop in each session.

Slide 4 – Title and Content Layout with a table

- Insert the following heading and table. Embolden and centre the heading and use a different font from the text in the table

Programme

Time	Lecture Hall (A)	Lecture Hall (B)
10.00–10.50am	A1	B1
11.00–11.50am	A2	B2
12.00–12.50pm	A3	B3
1.00–1.50pm	Lunch	Lunch
2.00–2.50pm	A4	B4
3.00–3.50pm	A5	B5

All Slides

- Apply a slide transition to all slides

Email

- Email a copy of your presentation to your teacher.

TASK 5 - Visiting Edinburgh

Use presentation software to create a slideshow for Edinburgh.

Slide 1 – Title Slide Layout

- Select an appropriate Design Theme
- Insert and centre the heading: HOLIDAY EDINBURGH. Use WordArt and apply animation
- Under the heading insert the text: Your guide to the most beautiful city in the world
- Insert a picture of Edinburgh sourced online in an appropriate place
- Animate the main heading and the graphic

Slide 2 – Two Content Layout with two columns

- Insert and centre the heading: EDINBURGH – SCOTLAND'S HISTORIC CAPITAL
- Below the heading insert the following text in two columns

Edinburgh Castle	Scott Monument
Royal Yacht Britannia	Royal Botanic Gardens
Palace of Holyrood house	Edinburgh Dungeon
Royal Mile	Our Dynamic Earth
Edinburgh Zoo	

- Insert a text box and centre the following text below these columns: Some of Edinburgh's top attractions

Slide 3 – Title Only Layout

- Insert and centre the heading: EDINBURGH CASTLE
- Insert the following passage on to the slide:
  See St Margaret's Chapel which is over 900 years old.
  Visit the Crown Room where you can see the Crown, Sceptre and Sword of State.
  Tour the Great Hall which houses a collection of weapons and armour.

Slide 4 – Title and Content Layout with a table

- Insert and centre the heading: ENTRANCE FEES
- Below the heading create the following table. Embolden the column headings and use a different font from the text in the rest of the table. Adjust the size of text as necessary

Attraction	Price per Adult	Family Ticket
Edinburgh Castle	£9.50	N/A
Our Dynamic Earth	£8.95	£16.50
Palace of Holyrood	£7.50	£19.00
Royal Yacht Britannia	£8.50	£23.00
Edinburgh Dungeon	£10.45	N/A

All Slides

- Apply a slide transition to all slides

Email

- Email a copy of your presentation to your teacher.

TASK 6 - Working from Home

Use presentation software to create a slideshow highlighting the benefits of working from home.

Slide 1 – Title Slide Layout

- Select an appropriate Design Theme
- Insert and centre the heading: HOMEWORKING. Use a large font size and apply animation
- Under the heading insert the text: Known as teleworking when it relies on the use of ICT
- Insert a suitable graphic sourced online in an appropriate place
- Animate the main heading and the graphic

Slide 2 – Two Content Layout with two columns

- Insert and centre the heading: ADVANTAGES OF HOMEWORKING
- Below the heading insert the following text in two columns

Reduction in floor space may lead to reduced costs	Avoidance of commuting – saving money
Floor space could be used for other purposes	Reduction in stress associated with travel
Improved motivation of homeworking staff	Working in comfort of own home
Increased productivity	More flexible working hours
Organisation can employ workers with special requirements who might not be able to work in the office	Greater job satisfaction

- Insert a text box and centre the following text below these columns: The effects of introducing homeworking on the organisation and the staff involved

Slide 3 – Title and Content Layout

- Insert and centre the heading: OCCUPATIONS WHERE HOMEWORKING IS POPULAR
- Insert the following passage on to the slide:
  The following are examples of occupations where homeworking is becoming increasingly commonplace:
  Computer consultants
  Writers and journalists
  Researchers
  Sales or marketing staff.

Slide 4 – Title and Content Layout with a table

- Insert and centre the heading: DISADVANTAGES OF HOMEWORKING
- Embolden the heading and use a different font from the text in the table.
- Below the heading centre the following table. Adjust the size of the text as necessary

To the Employee	To the Organisation
Feeling of isolation	Loss of management control
Difficulty in maintaining motivation	Cost of equipment
Difficulty in maintaining balance between life and work	Difficulty in providing on-the-job training
Social aspect of work is taken away from employee	Unavailability of staff for meetings to be called at short notice

All Slides

- Apply a slide transition to all slide

Email

- Email a copy of your presentation to your teacher.

EXTENSION TASK

TASK 7 - Health and Safety Legislation

Use presentation software to create a slideshow relating to health and safety in the workplace.

Slide 1 – Title Slide Layout

- Select an appropriate Design Theme
- Insert and centre the heading: HEALTH AND SAFETY. Use a large font size and apply animation
- Under the heading insert the text: A secure future for staff and customers
- Insert a suitable graphic sourced online in an appropriate place
- Animate the main heading and the graphic

Slide 2 – Two Content Layout with two columns

- Insert and centre the heading: ENSURING CONFIDENTIALITY OF INFORMATION
- Below the heading insert the following text in two columns:

Allocate passwords to computer users	Code and encrypt data
Control physical access to visitors	Return sensitive documents to their filing cabinets
Lock cabinets, doors and windows	Use dongles
Use voice prints and finger prints	Back up files

- Insert a text box and centre the following text below these columns: Some of the ways to ensure confidentiality and security of information

Slide 3 – Title and Content Layout with a bulleted list

- Insert and centre the heading: DATA PROTECTION
- Insert the following passage on to the slide:
  The Data Protection Act exists to protect personal privacy due to the amount of information held manually and on computer.
  Procedures must be in place to check, update or destroy inaccurate information.
  People must be told what use will be made of information held about them.
  Data must be obtained fairly and lawfully.
  Data must be accurate and kept up-to-date.

Slide 4 – Title and Content Layout with a table

- Insert and centre the heading: HEALTH AND SAFETY LEGISLATION
- Below the heading create the following table. Embolden column headings and use a different font from the text in the rest of the table. Adjust the size of the text as necessary.

Responsibilities of Employer	**Responsibilities of Employee**
Provide safe entrance and exit from work	Take reasonable care for his or her own health and safety
Ensure safe methods of working	Take reasonable care for the health and safety of other people
Provide training about health and safety	Cooperate with the employer or any other person appointed to carry out duties under the Act

All Slides

- Apply a slide transition to all slides

Email

- Email a copy of your presentation to your teacher.

BGE BUSINESS GLOSSARY TERMS

ADVERTISING
promotional displays used by businesses to inform consumers about the goods or services they sell

BANKRUPT
this is when a person or organisation is legally declared as unable to pay its debts

BRAND
a name, symbol, design (or a combination of all these) that the producer uses to make the product instantly recognisable

BUDGETING
this is how businesses manage money flowing into and out of the business

BUSINESS ETHICS
the values and principles which influence the business world and how businesses behave

CASH BUDGET
a plan of how much money you have and how you will spend it

CLOSING BALANCE
the amount of money in a bank account at the end of a period

CONSUMER
anyone who uses a good or service

CURRENT ACCOUNT
a type of bank account people and businesses use for day-to-day personal finances

CUSTOMER SERVICE
provision of service to a customer before, during and after a purchase

DEBT
a sum of money due or owed

DISCRIMINATION
the unjust or prejudicial treatment of people on the grounds of race, age, sex, or disability

DURABLE
long lasting so can be used many times

ECOMMERCE
buying and selling online

ENTREPRENEUR
an individual who creates and develops a business idea to produce a product or service that makes a profit

EQUALITY
equality is the right of everyone to equal treatment and opportunities, regardless of factors like gender, race and social position

ETHICAL BUSINESS
a business that considers the impact its actions, products and services have on the environment, people and animals

ETHICS
moral guidelines that tell us if what we are doing is right or wrong

EXCHANGE RATE
an exchange rate is a rate at which one country's currency will be exchanged for another

EXPORTS
exports are goods and services that are produced in one country and sold to buyers in another

FAIRNESS
the quality of treating people equally or in a way that is right or reasonable

FAIR TRADE
trade between companies in developed countries and producers in developing countries in which fair prices are paid to the producers

GAP IN THE MARKET
an idea for a product or service that is not currently being offered

GLOBALISATION
the term used to describe the fact that countries are increasingly working together and becoming more dependent on each other

GOVERNMENT
comprises Westminster Parliament (Houses of Parliament) and the Scottish Parliament

HIRE PURCHASE
hire purchase is when a business allows customers to purchase goods and pay for them in

instalments over an agreed period of time

IMPACT
the effect an action or policy has on people and society

IMPORTS
An import is a good or service bought in one country that was produced in another

INTANGIBLE
something that cannot be seen or touched

INTERNATIONAL TRADE
the process when countries buy and sell the goods and services they produce around the world

LEGISLATION
legislation is a law or a set of laws that have been passed by Parliament

GOODS
goods are tangible items and resources that satisfy people's needs and wants

INCOME
money received, especially on a regular basis, for work or through investments

JOB
a post of employment; full-time or part-time position

MARKET
a place where people exchange goods or services

MARKETING
the action or business of promoting and selling products or services, including market research and advertising

NEEDS
things required by people to survive such as water, shelter, food and clothing

NONDURABLE
something that is used up quickly

NON-GOVERNMENTAL ORGANISATION (NGO)
any non-profit, voluntary citizens' group that is organised on a local, national or international level

OPENING BALANCE
the amount of money in a bank account at the start of a period

PART-TIME WORKER
a part-time worker generally works fewer hours than their full-time equivalent

PLACE
where the customer can buy the product or service – how accessible it is

PRICE

the amount that a customer has to pay for a product or service

PRIMARY SECTOR

businesses in this sector use natural resources

PRODUCT

the good/service that is being sold

SAVINGS ACCOUNT

this is an account for saving money held at a bank or other financial institution and normally offers interest

SECTORS OF INDUSTRY

there are three sectors of industry: primary, secondary and tertiary

SECTORS OF THE ECONOMY

there are three sectors of the economy: the private sector, the public sector and the third, or voluntary, sector

SECONDARY SECTOR

businesses in this sector make or manufacture products

SERVICES

an act or use for which someone is willing to pay

SOCIAL BENEFITS

good things which happen to a local community as a result of a business

SOCIAL COSTS

the negative effects upon a local community that are caused as a direct result of a business.

SOCIAL RESPONSIBILITY

a policy which allows businesses to 'give something back' to the community, improve their image and reputation and correct any social costs it may have caused

TANGIBLE

something that can be seen and touched

TERTIARY SECTOR

businesses in this sector offer services, not products

TRAINING

the learning or teaching of a particular skill or expertise

WANTS

items that people would like to have but do not require for survival such as computers, jewellery and mobile phones

ZERO-HOURS CONTRACT WORKERS

workers who are not guaranteed set working hours but who instead get work when needed, so at certain 'busy periods' like during summer or Christmas